MONOGRAPHS OF THE
SOCIETY FOR RESEARCH IN
CHILD DEVELOPMENT

SERIAL NO. 210, VOL. 50, NO. 3

THE NEIGHBORHOOD WALK: SOURCES OF SUPPORT IN MIDDLE CHILDHOOD

BRENDA K. BRYANT
UNIVERSITY OF CALIFORNIA, DAVIS

WITH COMMENTARY BY
ROSS D. PARKE

MONOGRAPHS OF THE SOCIETY FOR RESEARCH IN CHILD
DEVELOPMENT, SERIAL NO. 210, VOL. 50, NO. 3

CONTENTS

ABSTRACT

BRYANT, BRENDA K. The Neighborhood Walk: Sources of Support in Middle Childhood. With Commentary by Ross D. PARKE. *Monographs of the Society for Research in Child Development*, 1985, **50**(3, Serial No. 210).

This report documents children's perception of their involvement with self-development, family members, and members of the community and begins to test the relation between that network and aspects of social-emotional functioning during middle childhood. Support was conceptualized to include experiences of both relatedness to and autonomy from others. Three major types of reported support in this study using the Neighborhood Walk were considered: others as resources (e.g., persons in the peer, parent, and grandparent generation; pets), intrapersonal sources of support (e.g., hobbies; fantasies—structured and unstructured; skill development), and environmental sources of support (e.g., places to get off to by oneself; formally sponsored organizations with structured and unstructured activities; informal, unsponsored meeting places).

One hundred sixty-eight children (72 7-year-olds and 96 10-year-olds), residing in nonmetropolitan and rural northern California and representing all but the lowest Hollingshead socioeconomic status, participated in this study. To assess their sources of support at home and in the neighborhood/community, each of these 168 children was taken on a Neighborhood Walk, and then several measures of social-emotional functioning were administered. Cross-sectional data form the empirical basis for a developmental perspective on sources of support, the structure of social-emotional functioning, and the relationship between sources of support and social-emotional functioning during middle childhood.

The child's perception of support was found relevant to predicting the social-emotional functioning of children growing up in relatively secure and low-stress conditions in modern American society. Furthermore, a broad-based as opposed to a limited network and informal as opposed to formal sources of support were more predictive of social-emotional functioning.

The empirical and theoretical relevance of considering middle childhood as a period of active development involving expansion and integration of social and affective phenomena was underscored by the results. First, it appears that the 7-year-olds have not yet developed the underlying response or habit clusters that characterize the 10-year-olds. Second, with respect to reported sources of support, 10-year-olds appear to have more elaborated sources of support than do 7-year-olds. Third, the findings confirm that developing a bridge to extended family and neighborhood resources is related to expressions of social-emotional functioning during middle childhood and that 10-year-olds appear to make effective use of more social support factors than do 7-year-olds. Finally, family size and sex of the child were key factors that interacted with specific types of support to predict social-emotional functioning.

I. THEORETICAL AND EMPIRICAL FRAMEWORK OF STUDY

In order to provide for the well-being of our children, more information is needed about their everyday sources of support. This was one of the conclusions of the Advisory Committee on Child Development (1976) in their report *Toward a National Policy for Children and Families.* The trends in the physical health and growth of American children are best known, while less is known regarding intellectual development and educational achievement, and least is known of the psychological well-being of and the conditions of social development for American children. Nowhere in the existing research literature is there a reasonably complete description of the actual social context of the daily lives of American children. The "Neighborhood Walk" was formulated as a procedure to assess the social context of developing children and to provide a means to study the relation of their sources of support to their social-emotional functioning.

Phenomenological considerations of children themselves form the foundation for the present perspective on sources of support in middle childhood. This report documents children's perception of their involvement with self-development, family members, and members of the community and begins to test the relation between that system and other aspects of social-emotional functioning.

Although it is of apparent concern to both children and adults, the nature and extent to which children have access to sources of support and the role of a network of support in social-emotional functioning in childhood have not been documented; this study begins to address these issues. The issue explored is the extent to which understanding the nature and extent of support presumably available during generally elusive but universal experiences of stress can predict social-emotional functioning during middle childhood. On the basis of the assumption that stress is universal and the need for support is fundamental to the development of all children, the present study considers the relevance of support in the social-emotional development of children growing up in relatively secure and low-stress conditions of modern American society.

The present research is based on the assumption that it will be useful to consider sources of support that extend beyond biological endowments and early mother-child relationships to help us understand the safety valves built into the conditions of human development. While most existing research on sources of support considers the role of support in high-stress conditions, the present research considers the theorized role of support in relation to the social-emotional functioning of children living with presumably low- or ordinary-stress conditions in relatively secure American environments and tests the assumption that a network of sources of support is predictive of these children's social-emotional functioning. Furthermore, it is hypothesized that a broad-based as opposed to a limited network (i.e., any one single factor) of support will be more predictive of social-emotional functioning. To this end, the present report provides the basis for considering childhood environments—including the grandparent generation (e.g., grandparents, neighbors who are older and no longer working), the parent generation (e.g., mothers, fathers, aunts, uncles, parents of peer playmates, teachers, librarians, shop owners), the peer generation (e.g., siblings, playmates), and the pet "generation" (e.g., own pet, neighborhood animals) as well as formal organizations and activities (e.g., 4-H clubs, Boy Scouts or Girl Scouts, church or temple) and informal organizations and activities (e.g., child-organized neighborhood "fort," homes of friends in which child is welcomed to play inside)—as they translate into social-emotional functioning of children. Both the value of particular sources of support and a network of sources of support will be explored as predictors of social-emotional functioning.

Sources of support will be considered from the perspective that support may stem from self or others, and consideration of developmental support will encompass experiences and opportunities for both autonomy and relatedness. To know, in developmental terms, the sources of expanding autonomy, we need to assess the sources of personal privacy, intimacy, and skill development; and to know, again in developmental terms, the sources of relatedness, we need to assess who provides both casual and intimate social exchanges in children's lives. The Neighborhood Walk provides the basis for these assessments, and this study assesses the predictive value of doing so in relation to social-emotional functioning.

That children receive an accentuated push or escape from the "nest" appears developmentally appropriate somewhere in the middle childhood years. That children have increasing access to others as sources of support (informal as well as formal) is also expected to show developmental variation. This study will specifically consider developmental differences by comparing reports of children in two age groups (7- and 10-year-olds) in middle childhood regarding their experiences of sources of support and how these reported experiences predict their views of themselves and others in social

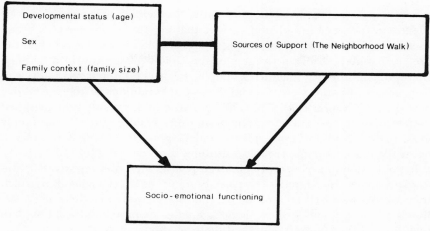

FIG. 1.—Summary model

situations. In addition, sex differences and the interaction of sex and age in the nature and extent of sources of support and their relation to social-emotional functioning will be explored. Finally, to understand the role of sources of support in social-emotional functioning more fully, it is considered important in this report to understand the family context in which children are operating. To do so, family network (i.e., family size) in particular will be taken into account.

In sum, this study presents the development of a method to assess sources of support from the child's perspective and tests the relevance of support for social-emotional functioning among children living in low-stress conditions and in so doing considers how children's developmental status (i.e., age), sex, and family context (i.e., family size) moderate the functional utility of these sources of support in predicting social-emotional functioning during middle childhood (see Fig. 1).

THE CHILD'S PERSPECTIVE

The Neighborhood Walk was designed to give children the opportunity to speak directly for themselves. It does not follow the tradition of relying on adult (e.g., parent, teacher, mental health worker) assessment of children's social and personal experiences (e.g., Achenbach & Edelbrock, 1978, 1981; Kogan, Smith, & Jenkins, 1977). This provides a stark contrast to the way children are typically included in surveys of American life-styles. Brim, for example, noticed that "children are treated merely as chattel or appendages of the household—the number of children is counted along with the number of automobiles, TV sets, and other household possessions" (1975, p. 522) in the large population surveys that are representative of a broad spectrum of American life-styles. Recently, Zill (1977) has documented the potential value and distinctiveness of the child's perspective in a national survey of children that included a sample of 2,301 children (aged 7–11) who were personally interviewed about the social conditions of their everyday lives (Brim, White, & Zill, 1978). The interviews in this survey were designed to determine the general environment in which children live—"their family lives, their friends, schools, health, and neighborhood activities—and to learn their perceptions, feelings, attitudes and values" (Zill, 1977, p. 1). What did these interviews with children reveal? First, Zill reports that children are more critical than their parents are of the neighborhoods in which they live. While nearly 60% of the parents interviewed rated their neighborhoods as "very good" or "excellent" as places to raise children, less than one-third of the children described their neighborhoods as "very good" or "excellent" places in which to grow up. In no one type of American community—city, suburb, town, or country—did a majority of the children interviewed rate their neighborhood as a "very good" or "excellent" place in which to grow up. When asked what changes would make the neighborhood "nicer for kids," the two most frequent changes identified were more and better places to play and less bad behavior and crime on the part of children and adults in the neighborhood. Other changes identified by the children include more children in the neighborhood to play with, cleaner neighborhoods with less pollution, improved traffic safety, and more beautiful neighborhoods (e.g., add trees, grass, flowers) (Zill, 1977). Although the adult perspective has traditionally been of interest to child development researchers, the findings from this survey, utilizing both child and adult reports, highlight that children can provide a perspective that is distinct from the parental viewpoint.

The present study considers the value of the child's perspective on his or her own sources of support to predicting aspects of social-emotional functioning in middle childhood. This approach to assessment of the child's sources of support rests on the phenomenological orientation that the individual's personal interpretations of the resources available at home and in the broader community are of utmost relevance to understanding how individuals interpret their own social experience and that of others. It is consistent with the earlier work of Bronfenbrenner (1977), Garbarino and Gilliam (1980), Lewin (1936), and Medrich, Roizen, Rubin, and Buckley (1982). Previous phenomenological research regarding available sources of support has focused on the perspective held by adolescents (Blyth, Hill, & Thiel, 1982) or adults/parents (e.g., Fischer et al., 1977; Garbarino & Gilliam, 1980; Polansky, Chalmers, Buttenwieser, & Williams, 1981). The present research extends the foundation of phenomenological considerations regarding the understanding of sources of support and psychological functioning to the middle childhood years.

SOURCES OF SUPPORT

Basis for Concern about Support

Not only is there a lack of documented information about the sources of support in children's lives, but there is also cause for concern as to the nature and extent of existing resources available to children in modern American society. This concern is reflected in the voices of both children and adults.

With respect to reports from children, current societal conditions in the United States appear to foster insecure, anxious children (Zill, 1979). Compared to children in two other highly industrialized and technologically advanced societies with democratic forms of government and capitalistic forms of economy (France and Japan), American children in middle childhood, more than their French and Japanese counterparts, feel anxious about their families as secure units (i.e., express worries about their families and fears about arguments between their parents). Concern about becoming a victim of a violent crime appears to be more universal, although Zill found that, among American children, this fear was more specific and more grounded in their own victimization experiences than was true of such fear among French or Japanese children. The concern for the need for support appears particularly salient when considering these reported fears and anxieties of American children.

In addition to concerns reported by children themselves in the national survey (Brim et al., 1978), changes in communities (e.g., suburbanization) and the increased fragmentation of family systems that have accompanied continued urbanization/suburbanization and mobility of families have raised concerns among adults about the social contexts available to today's children. Bronfenbrenner (1972) has argued that many factors conspire to isolate children from the rest of society, among which are the fragmentation of the extended family, the separation of residential and business areas, occupational mobility, consolidated schools, television, separate patterns of social life for different age groups, and the delegation of child care to specialists. These factors operate to decrease opportunity and incentive for meaningful contact between children and people older or younger than they are. Such changes appear to make parenting more difficult as well. Research has shown that, when factors conspire to isolate parents from the rest of society, the incidence of child abuse and neglect increases (Garbarino & Gilliam, 1980; Polansky et al., 1981). Thus considerations of modern societal trends suggest that children, for a variety of reasons, may not be experiencing the rich, extensive, and developmentally satisfying networks of support needed for social and emotional development.

The Developmental Importance of Support

Developing a bridge to community resources, having social supports, and having a feeling of group membership have been outlined as important for effective coping with stress situations (Caplan & Grunebaum, 1967; Hamburg & Adams, 1967; Rapaport, 1962; Viney, 1976). Research considering the value of sources of support has consequently focused mostly on the role of support in moderating stressful conditions. Zelkowitz (1978) tested the hypothesis that, given a highly stressed (e.g., low income, urban environment) and/or depressed mother, the presence of other support figures will serve to decrease the likelihood that a child will exhibit poor social adjustment. She found that those children (in highly stressful family situations) with more available supportive figures had fewer reported behavior problems. Similarly, Werner and Smith (1982) report that the overwhelming majority (80%) of resilient youths who grew up in chronic poverty felt that support and counsel from informal sources of community support (friends and parent figures) had been useful and reported a greater number and availability of these informal sources of support than did youths with serious coping problems. Jersild (1947) also demonstrated that ordinarily occurring fears of children were made worse when the children were alone. In other words, access to support is seen as important for human development because it is thought to mitigate the negative consequences of stressful conditions and to enhance welcomed social-emotional development.

In addition to societal changes and the increased stressfulness of life for children in modern American society, however, the study of sources of support in relation to social-emotional functioning and development is of value. First, one can argue that it is impossible to be open, free, and caring within oneself and within the family while remaining emotionally insulated from the wider world outside (Conger, 1981). In other words, sources of support are critical to psychological functioning for all humans, with the importance of sources of support increasing with increasing stressfulness in an individual's life (Conger, 1981; Garbarino & Gilliam, 1980).

Second, it can be argued that stress in conjunction with appropriate support is critical to enhancing social-emotional development. Erikson (1950) views social-emotional development as centered around crises and stressful ambiguity in conjunction with the individual's inner resources and external appropriately supportive figures. Piaget (1932) considers intellectual conflict as the foundation for enhanced social reasoning. Empirical studies, too, indicate that psychological well-being is not simply inversely related to stressful experiences (Bradburn, 1969). For example, Elder's (1974) study of youths during the Great Depression and their continued development into adulthood showed that offspring of deprived families under certain conditions of support developed particularly satisfying social-emotional lives. Stress and the relevant support through individual abilities and/or the resources of others may be viewed as the central elements that make possible social-emotional development.

While it is being argued that access to support is important for healthy development, little is known about the nature and extent of support that is most likely to be used and conducive to enhanced social-emotional development. In the process of conducting a longitudinal study, Werner and Smith (1977) sent letters with suggestions for follow-up and referrals to special agencies to the parents of all 10-year-old children identified as at risk. At the 18-year-old follow-up, only a third of all the youths at risk at age 10 had received some professional help or psychotherapy, and less than half the youths considered at age 10 to be in need of long-term mental health services had encountered professional intervention. Of the youths with serious learning or mental health problems in middle childhood who did receive some form of professional help, less than half improved between the ages of 10 and 18. Furthermore, of all sources of acknowledged help, peer friends were preferred to both parents and professionals by the youths studied, especially by the youths with long-term mental health problems. Among these youths with learning and behavior problems diagnosed in childhood, it was found that professionals (whether teachers, counselors, ministers, psychologists, psychiatrists, or social workers) were ranked far below peers, parents, and older friends as sources of help to whom the youths would spontaneously turn. These findings provided by Werner and Smith (1977) make a strong argument for identifying existing informal sources of support within the child's immediate environment and indicate the need to consider both peer- and parent-generation sources of support.

Recognizing also that sources of support need not be planned agents of intervention or socialization, pet support will be considered in addition to human support. Indeed, Lago, Baskey, Green, and Hand (1981) propose that a pet can be a confidant, a source of humor, a nonjudgmental companion, a source of shared daily activities and responsibilities, and a constantly available companion that can be a powerful aid in promoting desired kinds of behavior (Lago, Knight, & Connell, 1982). On the basis of the above considerations, both formally and informally sponsored organizations and activities will be considered as potentially valuable sources of support, and these will be categorized, when relevant, according to generation (peer, parent, grandparent, or pet). Furthermore, it is hypothesized that the informal sources of support (including pets) will be more predictive of social-emotional functioning than will the formal sources.

Concept of Support

Earlier sections of this report have emphasized the value of others as support and have alluded to the role of the individual's own abilities and personal resources in promoting social-emotional development. Certainly issues of relatedness are of central importance to developmental psychologists since the very survival of a human organism requires human bonding and attachment formation with at least one nurturing other. The need for relatedness remains with us throughout the life cycle, although the nature and extent of this relatedness to others varies with developmental stages or issues. Equally important for growth and development is the competing developmental requirement of separateness from others and development of autonomous functioning, initially a matter of adequate integration of basic vegetative functions (Murphy, 1974). The very essence of most views of child development in our society argues for the importance of the development of both autonomy and satisfying social relationships with others for healthy development (Wolfe, 1978).

Available empirical research supports the importance of considering both autonomy from and relatedness to others as supportive of social-emotional functioning. For example, research has indicated that being in nonchosen continual presence of others does not support satisfying social interaction, whereas experiences with chosen aloneness (i.e., experiences of autonomy) can promote subsequent satisfying social interaction (Wolfe, 1978). Werner and Smith (1982) also report that vulnerable but resilient children, even in the early years of childhood, appear to balance a strong social orientation and social competence with a great deal of autonomy and independence.

The need for autonomy may be expressed differently at varying stages of the human life cycle (Schwartz, 1968). Some form of supervision, even if from a distance, is typically considered important to children in middle childhood. Consequently, separation issues during middle childhood may center on opportunities for distant adult/parental supervision and access to experiences and individuals outside the parental home base. In addition, the degree to which activities of developing personal interests and skills are structured can reflect the degree to which children are given the autonomy to structure their own experiences and development. Aspects of autonomy must be seen, then, in contexts in which adults often impose at least limited supervision over children.

Issues of both autonomy from and relatedness to others operate in intimate relationships. Intimacy has been conceptualized as one of four basic states of privacy (Proshansky, Ittelson, & Rivlin, 1972) and, as protected communication, serves a critical function of autonomy (Westin, 1967). At the same time, intimacy signals a very special kind of interpersonal relatedness that is thought to satisfy unique needs (Caplan, 1974), in particular, the need for sharing with someone while withholding (or remaining autonomous) from others. In a study with seventh graders, Blyth (1982) found that, of all the people identified by these youths as important in their lives, only 27% of the important people offered intimate encounters (i.e., encounters in which the youths reported sharing their feelings a lot). Intimate relations are not characteristic of all important relations but can be considered as expressions of issues involving both relatedness and autonomy and, as such, will be differentiated from nonintimate relatedness to others.

In sum, support is conceptualized to include both experiences of relatedness to others and experiences of autonomy from others. This is a more comprehensive view of support than those that traditionally focus solely on the need for relatedness to others.

MODERATING FACTORS

Developmental Status in Relation to Support

Concern in the empirical and theoretical literature regarding social-emotional development of children and youths has focused on early childhood and adolescence to the neglect of middle childhood, otherwise labeled the latency stage of development (Scarr, 1979). This study will consider two age groups typically viewed as part of the "latency" period and, in so doing, will provide a basis for generating an empirical framework for future developmental studies of middle childhood.

The ability to influence positively one's external environment has been conceptualized by some (e.g., Dabrowski, 1964) as indicating the capacity of the individual to develop. Consider that as the child develops the complexity of the child's life ordinarily increases: the child does more, with more people, and in more places (Garbarino & Gilliam, 1980). Furthermore, as people move through different stages of the life cycle, they continually establish new sets of social relationships that, at least in part, serve to define particular stages in the life cycle (Blyth, 1982). Relationships and involvements in activities that are developmentally appropriate in the lives of young children, for example, are thought to lose their meaning and appropriateness for teenagers (Polansky et al., 1981). With respect to middle childhood, the

10-year-old is seen as influencing many adults (not just parents) and other children (not simply siblings) in many settings (not simply in the home) and as having many ways of communicating (not simply cries, eye contact, and smiles) (Garbarino & Gilliam, 1980). School-aged children, in comparison to infants, have been viewed in particular as having extended areas of activities and autonomy (e.g., crossing the street, going to school, visiting friends) because of their greater freedom of movement (Lewin, 1951). The 10-year-old is viewed as significantly more limited, though, than the adolescent (Garbarino & Gilliam, 1980). Based on the existing age contrasts cited, it is hypothesized that, with age, children will have more complex and expanded networks of support and that, with increasing access to autonomy and relatedness to others, sources of support will predict social-emotional functioning better for older than for younger children in middle childhood.

Sex Differences in Relation to Support

Not only is age or stage of development anticipated as relevant to the nature and extent of sources of support garnered, but sex differences are anticipated as well. Wolfe (1978) summarizes existing research on sex differences in middle childhood with respect to use of space in and outside the family home. Consistent sex differences have emerged. Beginning at about 9 years of age, boys, as compared to girls of the same age, are allowed to go further from the home without asking permission (Hart, 1978). Landy (1959) reports that mothers are more likely to check up on their daughters than on their sons when their children are playing outdoors. Thus it is hypothesized that boys will report involvement with more neighbors and neighborhood organizations than will girls.

Not only have sex differences emerged in children's use of space outside the home, but also age and sex appear to interact such that sex differences increase as the age of the child advances (Moore & Young, 1978). Consequently, where sex differences occur, it is hypothesized that these differences are greater at age 10 than they are at age 7.

Additionally, while males may have greater access to their neighborhoods than females do, the kinds of supportive relationships the two sexes develop are expected to differ as well. Specifically, existing research suggests that males seek out more extensive, less intimate relationships than do females (Berndt, 1981; Waldrop & Halverson, 1975). Thus it is hypothesized that males will report more casual relationships and fewer intimate relationships than females will.

Finally, there is empirical research that documents that boys and girls are differentially sensitive to particular caretaker strategies and characteristics (Baumrind, 1975; Werner & Smith, 1982). Thus even if boys and girls receive the same support, different outcomes in social-emotional functioning are expected. More specifically, it is hypothesized that the sex of a child will moderate the relation between sources of support and social-emotional functioning.

Family Context in Relation to Support

Family size is particularly salient when considering the possible support available in the family and the possible support needed outside the immediate family. It has been observed by several researchers that families implicated in child neglect and/or abuse cases are likely to have more children than those in comparison groups do (Giovannoni & Billingsley, 1970; Polansky et al., 1981; Wolock & Horowitz, 1979; Young, 1964). The fact of having many children has the potential to increase frustrations for parents when they are trying to deal with the complexities of meeting the needs of individual children (Kidwell, 1981). Having a larger number of siblings has been found to be related to perceptions of greater parental punitiveness and weaker parental supportiveness (Kidwell, 1981). Indeed, children from large families may have greater need of supportive figures to supplement the support they can garner from parents who are more often overloaded by needs of others than do children from small families. Thus it is hypothesized that the sources of support garnered by children in large families will differ from those garnered by children in small families and that family size will moderate the relation between sources of support and social-emotional functioning.

SOCIAL-EMOTIONAL FUNCTIONING

Social-emotional functioning addresses the important issue of how children think and feel about themselves and others. Social-emotional functioning in this report includes measures of internal experiencing (e.g., empathy) as well as social skill development (e.g., social perspective taking) and, as such, is intended to highlight the basis for shared interests between clinical child psychologists and basic child development researchers. Whereas clinical researchers have historically been apt to study the development of psychopathology rather than the development of prosocial functioning (Garmezy, 1982; Murphy, 1962), basic child development researchers have been reluctant to tread outside traditional experimental methods (McCall, 1977) and examine those aspects of child development that are not directly manipulable or directly observable by the researcher. Phenomenological concerns are particularly characteristic of the interests of clinicians. More

11

specifically, clinical concerns almost always include considerations of the internal experiencing of the child. It is not sufficient to be concerned that children come to understand the thoughts and feelings of others objectively and behave prosocially. Rather how children feel about themselves in relation to others as well as their actual social skills are of equal concern.

Social-emotional functioning, then, in this report includes measures of children's internal experiencing of themselves in relation to others as well as social skill development. This perspective is intended to help bridge communication between clinicians working with children in applied settings and the more basic child development researchers.

SUMMARY

It is argued that we need to understand and appreciate, from the child's perspective, the relatively enduring aspects of the day-to-day social and personal environment children experience and its relevance to social-emotional functioning in middle childhood. This study presents the development of a method to assess sources of support for social-emotional functioning among children living in low-stress conditions and in so doing considers how children's developmental status (i.e., age), sex, and family context (i.e., family size) moderate the functional utility of these sources of support in predicting social-emotional functioning during middle childhood. The building of this knowledge base is intended to provide an informed foundation for the creation of developmentally responsive environments for school-aged children. Increased understanding of the development and relationship of the developing child's perceived ecological support systems holds promise for more effective formulation of the process of social-emotional development as regards potential sources of support within the child's own sustaining environment. Overall, the purpose of this report is to present the Neighborhood Walk and to help redress the current limitation of existing knowledge and methodology regarding the developmental assessment of childhood sources of support and its relation to social-emotional functioning.

The following hypotheses were considered. (1) The child's perception of sources of support is relevant to predicting the social-emotional functioning of children growing up in relatively secure and low-stress conditions in modern American society. (2) A network of support is more predictive of social-emotional functioning than is any one single factor of support. (3) Informal sources of support will be more predictive of social-emotional functioning than will the formal sources. (4) Children's developmental status, sex, and family context will be related to the extent of support garnered and will moderate the functional utility of sources of support in predicting social-emotional functioning during middle childhood; more specifically, (a) with age, children will have more complex and expanded networks of support, (b) the sources of support will predict social-emotional functioning better for older than for younger children, (c) boys will report involvement with more neighbors and neighborhood organizations than will girls, (d) boys will report more casual relationships and fewer intimate relationships than will females, (e) where sex differences occur, differences will be greater at age 10 than at age 7, (f) the sex of the child will moderate the relationship between sources of support and social-emotional functioning, (g) sources of support garnered by children in large families will differ from those garnered by children in small families, and (h) family size will moderate the relationship between sources of support and social-emotional functioning.

II. RATIONALE FOR THE NEIGHBORHOOD WALK

The Neighborhood Walk developed in this study concerns itself with reported sources of support available to the child within his or her family, neighborhood, and community. The Neighborhood Walk does not arbitrarily define territorial limits of the child's neighborhood. Rather a range of places and activities, both formal and informal, that were thought to be potential sources of support to children's needs for autonomy and relatedness during middle childhood was assessed, as was the accessibility of these opportunities. More specifically, this Neighborhood Walk assesses how children vary in their access to, interaction with, and use of themselves (i.e., intrapersonal sources of support), friends and relatives (i.e., others as resources), and recreational facilities (i.e., environmental sources of support) in their communities. Both casual versus intimate and formal versus informal relationships are considered. The method relies on the children's report of their own experiences, and in this unique perspective lies its strength. The Neighborhood Walk is aimed at the assessment of the child's personal experience of sources of support and, as such, is not a collective, sociological measure of neighborhoods but rather an individual, psychological "landscape" of sources of support. In other words, the neighborhood experience in this interview focuses on potential sources of support for social-emotional development during middle childhood as viewed by the child during a walk in his or her own home neighborhood.

ENVIRONMENTAL SOURCES OF SUPPORT

It can be argued that children are the primary consumers of residential neighborhoods. On the basis of week-long diary records of 10- and 11-year-olds in England, it was determined that most children this age spend 6–14 hours per week or 1–2 hours daily outdoors, primarily in their own neighborhoods (Himmelweit, Oppenheim, & Vince, 1958). Not only do children spend a fair amount of time in the community, but also multiethnic data provided by 8- to 12-year-old children in identifying their favorite places, where they go after school or during weekends, "emphasized children's closest friends, together with their home, the surrounding streets and immediately accessible places such as schools, parks, playgrounds, stores, and community facilities" (Moore & Young, 1978, p. 106). It has been argued that children have an overwhelming need to engage in activities outside their homes, both because homes do not afford enough space or privacy and because their games and explorations produce adventures requiring expansive and challenging settings (Medrich et al., 1982). As such, Coates and Bussard (1974) suggest that children are the most important and least represented users of planned residential environments.

At the same time, children do not define their neighborhoods and play areas by the same boundaries that city planners employ (Marcus, 1974; Maurer & Baxter, 1972). The child's perspective of neighborhood differs from that of the adult. Marcus notes the phenomenon of little-used play equipment in formal, professionally designed, residential playground settings. Instead children use the "entire" neighborhood for play, not just the formally designated "play area" on the site plan. Maurer and Baxter, in another example, found that elementary school–aged children in their study conceived of their neighborhoods as approximately .67 square blocks, an area considerably smaller than what city planners define as a neighborhood. In other words, how children perceive and make use of basic, physical aspects of their neighborhoods is not well understood by the adults who have children's interests in mind.

What Moore and Young (1978) report as most salient about the physical aspects of the child's reported environment are immediately accessible places in the neighborhood. How children experience their neighborhoods and extrafamilial sources of support, then, is deemed to be influenced by the accessibility of such experiences. Accessibility in this study was measured by the repeated use of the following question: "To [do that], do you walk, ride a bike, or go by car or bus?" In this way the Neighborhood Walk was designed to consider the environmental factor of accessibility of children's sources of support.

Accessibility to support can also, in part, reflect the adult sector's commitment to the young (Medrich et al., 1982). Community pools, parks, school yards, libraries, and country clubs offer examples of formal, adult-sponsored organizations with opportunities for unstructured activities for children. Organizations like Little League, Brownies or Cub Scouts, and 4-H represent formal, adult-sponsored organizations with extensive opportunities for structured activities for children. Adult commitment to children, however, need not be formal. Informal, unsponsored meeting places are those more private meeting grounds with relatively unsupervised (i.e., unsupervised by adults) activities. Examples of these privately (informally)

15

sponsored places include homes a child is allowed to enter and play in, neighborhood clubs, which typically use family yards or garages, and child-built forts in the neighborhood. These places and activities typically involve adult sanction of children's use of space as well as distant rather than direct adult supervision. The Neighborhood Walk was designed to assess both formal and informal sponsoring of children's meeting and "get-away" places and their value in relation to social-emotional functioning.

In sum, the Neighborhood Walk yields categories that assess a child's access to independence (i.e., places to get off to alone) as well as to places to join others in both formally sponsored organizations (both structured and unstructured) and informal, unsponsored meeting places. In addition, the accessibility of interpersonal and intrapersonal support is assessed.

INTERPERSONAL ENVIRONMENT—OTHERS AS SUPPORT

Not only can environments be characterized by physical dimensions, but the social properties of environments can be useful to consider as well (Proshansky et al., 1972). As was the case with the physical aspects of children's neighborhood environments, little is known about the child's imagery of his or her interpersonal environment. Neighborhood attachment to others may develop from several sources, ranging from informal, casual neighboring (e.g., talking with neighbors) to special friends (e.g., adults at library, church, store, etc. with whom child has special talks) to intimate confidants (e.g., people with whom child shares worries, secrets, sadnesses, and angers). Rubin (1980) observes that this specialization and differentiation of relationships (e.g., casual vs. intimate friendship) begins early in life. In fact, the neighborhood has been viewed as the primary social context for families with young children (Garbarino & Gilliam, 1980) and, as such, the primary context for considering the development of specialized and differentiated relationships. Families with children have been found to be most strongly connected to the neighborhood (to local institutions, local kin, and local acquaintances) (Fischer et al., 1977). From the interpersonal perspective, children again seem to be primary consumers of neighborhoods.

It has been found that involvement with others and accessibility to them depends, in part, on population-density factors (Rubin, 1980; van Vliet, 1981). For example, van Vliet found that children living in urban environments had more child friends than did children in suburban environments and that the number of friends correlated positively with the child density in the neighborhood. Not only may population density influence the extent to which others are available to children, but cultural, familial, and sociostructural factors can also operate to inhibit or encourage the development of social ties with others (Medrich et al., 1982; Rubin, 1980; van Vliet, 1981).

The present study is concerned with the extent to which others are experienced as available and accessible to the children interviewed. Because there are a number of complex factors that can influence the extent to which children experience interpersonal relations, the Neighborhood Walk methodology allows these factors to operate and in doing so enhances capturing individual differences of children's experiences of "neighborhood" resources.

Developmental considerations may also operate in determining the social involvement with others in the neighborhood. Blyth (1982) contends that, as individuals move through different stages of the life cycle, they take on new sets of social relationships, which, at least in part, serve to define particular stages in the life cycle. The complexity of the child's changing social world during middle childhood is little understood, although it is generally thought that, with age, children become increasingly peer oriented. The nature, complexity, and accessibility of children's social environment at two different age groups were taken into account as the Neighborhood Walk was developed and were allowed to vary in content and extent.

In sum, the Neighborhood Walk yields categories to assess peer-, parent-, grandparent-, and pet-generation sources of support. Included in each of these categories are subcategories that differentiate casual versus intimate relationships (e.g., know and interact with peers vs. intimate talks with peers). Also included as support from others was a child's degree of involvement with his or her parents' world of work (e.g., can reach parent at work by phone vs. actually helps parent at work).

INTRAPERSONAL ENVIRONMENT

Not only do children operate in physical and interpersonal environments, but they also have an ongoing interpretation of their place in the environment. A concern for the intrapersonal environment in the Neighborhood Walk takes two forms: specifically, as sources of internal support and, more broadly, as phenomenological reporting throughout the Neighborhood Walk method. This overriding concern for the child's inner perspective has been previously discussed.

The interest in specific internal sources of concern requires some introduction. As a specific interest, internal/intrapersonal support is viewed in the present study as psychological experiences that can serve to buffer the individual from internal or external stresses and/or provide a basis for enhanced participation in the physical and interpersonal realms of the child's environment. Although clinicians have traditionally been keenly interested in selected aspects of children's internal support networks (e.g., fantasies), with the exception of considering the effects of television (i.e., structured fantasy) on children (Liebert, Neale, & Davidson, 1973), research has not clearly documented the role of internal support in relation to the social-emotional functioning of children. In this report, fantasies, hobbies, and experiences of skill attainment form the basis for considering internal sources of support.

Thus the Neighborhood Walk yields categories to assess a child's involvement with hobbies, fantasies (both structured ones such as those presented by viewing television and unstructured ones such as make-believe friends), and skill development (e.g., music lessons) and the public display of skills (e.g., participation in a church or community play or program).

Finally and more broadly, the Neighborhood Walk is aimed at the assessment of the child's personal experiences of sources of support and, as such, is not a collective measure of neighborhoods. In other words, having a park in one's neighborhood is not considered relevant to a particular child's neighborhood network of environmental support if the child does not report using it. The Neighborhood Walk method represents a phenomenological perspective that assumes that the aspects of the environment that operate most powerfully in the course of child development are those aspects of the environment actually perceived and given meaning by the child (Blyth, 1982; Blyth et al., 1982; Bronfenbrenner, 1979; Garbarino, Burston, Raber, Russell, & Crouter, 1978; Lewin, 1951).

ASSESSMENT TECHNIQUES

This interest in the psychological reality has been particularly represented in existing research aimed at the assessment of the child's interpersonal environment (Blyth, 1982; Blyth et al., 1982; Garbarino et al., 1978). These researchers have asked adolescents to identify individuals with whom they experience certain kinds of relationships. Again, it appears that the child (adolescent) perspective differs from that of the adult (parent), although there can be substantial overlap in perspectives. Children and their mothers from three different home settings (suburban, urban, and rural) showed 39.9%–57.1% overlap in their identification of the "top ten" people whom the child knew best or who knew the child best (Garbarino et al., 1978). Interviewing approaches to the interpersonal aspects of children's environments vary as well in how open ended versus structured they are. The most open-ended question used to date has been Garbarino et al.'s initial probe of "make a list of the people you know best or who know you best, outside your immediate family" (1978, p. 420). Structuring the child's response followed as the child was then asked to narrow this list down to the top ten of "really significant others." This procedure focuses generally on one kind of relationship (i.e., knowing well) and arbitrarily limits the number of very significant others. Blyth et al. (1982) structured their interview along two dimensions: varying kinds of relationships (e.g., people you spend time with or do things with; people you go to for advice) and varying contexts (e.g,, family, school, neighborhood). Blyth et al.'s procedure was open ended in that they did not arbitrarily limit the number of significant others identified and in that they also elicited important others who did not fit the researcher's categories but whom the adolescent experienced as significant others. Since very general questions are open to a variety of interpretations, adding structure in the manner of Blyth et al. helped make the task more uniform across subjects. While the value of open-ended questions is to heighten the child's participation in defining the task and giving answers that are particularly relevant to himself or herself, the value of structure is generally to ensure comparable consideration of all relevant topics by all individuals interviewed. A combination of structured and open-ended questions is aimed at achieving some of the benefits of each approach in the Neighborhood Walk. One unique form of a combined structured and open-ended format used in the Neighborhood Walk structures the context of the interview in the child's own neighborhood. Each interview begins in the child's front yard, then progresses along a path of the child's choice, and returns to the child's home by the time the child is directly asked questions about his or her immediate neighbors. Such an approach is aimed at engaging the child in activity relevant to the interview and eliciting meaningful cues regarding children's experiences in their home neighborhoods.

While open-ended interviews have largely been used to obtain elaborated notions of the social and psychological significance of aspects of the individual's neighborhoods, such approaches are particularly sensitive to interviewer skill (Maurer & Baxter, 1972), so both quantity and quality of data across subjects are subject to wide-ranging "interviewer error." Standardized definitions of words as well as introductory and follow-up questions to open-ended questions help reduce interviewer differences. All three practices were used in the development of the Neighborhood Walk.

In addition to interviewer error, there is always the question of the reliability with which individuals respond to questions, and the issue of reliability of responses tends to increase as we move downward in age of the interviewee. Zill (1979) has documented this difficulty in conducting surveys involving children. In the national survey of children, he reports that lack of truthfulness as a source of unreliability does not appear more characteristic of children than of their parents. It appears, though, that children are less consistent in their responses than adults are. The type of question asked of children also appears to influence the reliability over time of the answer. Vaillancourt (1973) found that the more personal and concrete the subject matter on which children were questioned, the more stable their responses.

With issues of reliability of child responses considered, Zill (in press) argues convincingly that the limitations posed by the lesser stability of child reports are more than compensated for by our opportunity to develop the sometimes unique perspective of the child, a perspective that is often a fresh and provocative message about children themselves, about their families, and about our society.

Nonetheless, multiple sources of perspectives on neighborhoods are warranted for a comprehensive understanding of child environments. Such additional sources primarily come, when feasible, by two means: first, participant observation (Lomnitz, 1977; Spencer, 1964; Stack, 1974) and nonparticipant observation (Barker & Wright, 1951; Zelkowitz, 1978) (i.e., naturalistic observation) and, second, interviews with adults about their children's experiences (e.g., Zelkowitz, 1978). Since this study does not comprise such complementary methods, care was taken in the development of the Neighborhood Walk to offer the child concrete cues of neighborhood settings by walking in areas pertaining to questions whenever possible. For example, when asking about specific neighbors, the interviewer had the child point out the neighbor's home. Follow-up questions were also developed in the Neighborhood Walk to encourage thoughtful answers. For example, children were asked not only if they knew their neighbors but also what the names of these known neighbors were. Not only were children asked if neighbors talked with them, but also, in a follow-up to an affirmative answer on this question, they were asked when they last talked. A last example of this follow-up procedure used throughout the Neighborhood Walk is that, when children reported a neighborhood pet to be a special friend, they were asked what made the pet special. In lieu, then, of multiple informants regarding a particular child's environment, multiple questions (e.g., introductory as well as follow-up questions) and cues (e.g., visual and kinesthetic) were used to elicit thoughtful and reliable interviews from the participants in this study.

III. METHOD

SAMPLE

One hundred and sixty-eight children (i.e., "target" children) participated in this project. Of these 168, 72 had just finished the first grade, and 96 had just finished the fourth grade. The *mean age* of the "first graders" was 7-3, and the mean age of the "fourth graders" was 10-3. In the remainder of this *Monograph*, the first graders are referred to as 7-year-olds and the fourth graders as 10-year-olds; the terms are interchangeable. Equal numbers of boys and girls in each age group were included.

The *family context* was considered in the selection of the children for this study. Family size, sibling age, and sibling sex were assessed. In particular, within each age group, equal numbers of children were selected from small families (i.e., two-child families) and large families (i.e., three-or-more-child families). Eighty-two percent of these large families contained three or four children. The remaining 18% were very large families with five to eight children. According to chi-square analyses, these very large families were not unevenly distributed between the 7- and 10-year-old groups and between the male and female target child groups. Furthermore, each child in the study had an older sibling, a brother or sister who was 2–3 years older than the target child. Equal numbers of these older siblings were brothers and sisters for each age group, family size, and sex of the target child. Although not of major interest in this study, sex of sibling is treated as a control factor in future analyses.

Family units included in this study were relatively stable as well. Only children who had continuous contact with two parents were included. Accordingly, 164 of the 168 families had both parents living at home with no step-parents involved. The four remaining families included two families with recently separated parents and two families with divorced parents. All four of these altered family arrangements consisted of both mothers and fathers who participated with their children on a regular, ongoing weekly if not daily basis.

Parental age can be considered a rough indicator of developmental readiness for the demands of parenting experienced by the parents of the sample interviewed. At the time of the birth of the children in this study, parental age was typically in the twenties. The mean age of the mothers at the time of this study was 36, and the mean age of the fathers was 38. Both of these age distributions had a standard deviation of about 4 years. For the 7-year-olds, the mean age of the mothers was 33-10 (SD = 3-8), and the mean age of the fathers was 36-10 (SD = 4-4). For the 10-year-olds, the mean age of the mothers was 37-7 (SD = 4-6), and the mean age of the fathers was 39-8 (SD = 4-10).

The *community context* deserves attention as well. All children were residing in nonmetropolitan and rural northern California at the time of their participation. Based on 1980 census information, the mean total population density (persons per square kilometer) of the census tracts represented in this study was 122 (SD = 153). The average child (5–14 years of age) density was 90 (SD = 59), and older adult (65 years and older) density was 22 (SD = 32). In other words, children were living in generally low to moderate population-density conditions. More specifically, the participating children resided in one of six counties, with the majority (87%) living in one county. In this county, eight towns were represented with populations ranging in size from 40 to 36,000. The county seat of this county, Community CS, contributed the most subjects and represented 44% of the sample. A university town, Community U, contributed another 39% of the sample. The remaining 17% predominantly represented a more rural setting, Community R, surrounding these two larger towns. All three settings support agricultural concerns of a northern California agricultural center. Community U is a university community with a major college of agriculture and environmental sciences and cooperative extension outreach program. Community CS is a central agricultural and marketing center (e.g., processing plants, major transportation center) and historically provides support services (e.g., hospitals) to the central valley agricultural community. The more rural areas surrounding these two towns provide "country homes" for professionals working in the larger towns as well as for others more directly involved in agricultural development and marketing. Finally, people in all three communities have easy access (i.e., less than 2 hours by car) to two major urban areas (i.e., the state capital and San Francisco).

Furthermore, with the exception of the mobility of university students in Community U, these *communities are stable.* On the basis of 1980 census tract data encompassing all the tracts represented by children interviewed in this study, it was determined that 77% of the population in Community CS, 38% of the population in Community U, and 77% of the population in Community R had been living in the same county 5 years earlier. With the exception of a mobile student population, these communities reflect considerable proportions of families with an apparent commitment to living in these communities. This was certainly true for most of the families represented in this study. The mean number of years that the mothers of the children in this study reported living at their current address was 5.92 (SD = 4.18), and the mean number of years in the current county was 13.91 (SD = 10.23). In sum, most of the children in the sample had experienced relative stability of community in growing up.

Those children who had experienced moves had, nonetheless, had a steady experience with rural or nonmetropolitan settings. Eighty-two percent of the mothers of children in this study reported that the target child had spent most of his or her childhood in a community of more than 10,000 but less than 50,000 people; another 16% reported that the target child had lived most of his or her life in a community of less than 10,000 (actually, half of these had spent their time in communities of less than 2,500); and the remaining 2% of the sample had spent most of their lives in communities with more than 50,000. Steady experience with rural/nonmetropolitan environments was definitely the norm for children in this study.

With respect to *socioeconomic status* (SES), the father's educational level and employment status (one unemployed father) were considered in combination according to the Hollingshead (1965) schema. Hollingshead SES levels potentially range from 1 to 5, with the lower end of the scale representing high SES. In the present sample, SES scores ranged from 1 to 4 (*M* = 2.38, SD = .98). Although SES and family size can be related, in the present study SES did not differentiate the small families from the large families. Although neither parental educational level nor parental employment status was a criteria for screening potential interviewees, the lowest SES level was not found in this sample. Yamamoto, Acosta, and Evans (1982) note that, while persons in both class 4 and class 5 represent the working class and the poor, respectively, individuals in class 4 have considerably more opportunity than those in class 5 do to achieve middle-class possessions and goals. In other words, although the families in this study could have been economically stressed, they were in a position to achieve according to middle-class values.

As is characteristic for the majority of mothers of school-aged children today (Hoffman, 1979), in this sample *a majority of the mothers were employed* (65%). There was no significant difference in the number of mothers in small versus large families who were employed. The percent of maternal employment is within 1 standard deviation of the mean 70% (SD = 5) of women with children aged 6–17 who, according to 1980 census data, are in the labor force in the census tracts represented in this study. More specifically, the 65% figure for the present sample is within 1 standard deviation of the relevant mean percentage for Community CS (*M* = 70, SD = 5) and Community R (*M* = 64, SD = 9) and is within 2 standard deviations of the mean 76% (SD = 7) for Community U. Twenty-two percent worked full-time, while another 43 percent worked part-time.

Another measure of community context has to do with accessibility of *community resources.* All the families in this study owned at least one car. The mean number of cars owned per family was 2.10 (SD = .74). Almost all the parents in these families reported that they had access to a car virtually all the time (95% of the mothers and 97% of the fathers). Parents, then, at least had reasonable access to community resources.

With respect to *housing conditions,* the mean number of rooms per home was 7.68 (SD = 1.64), and the mean number of people per home was 4.84 (SD = 1.15). Only 35% of the children in this sample shared a bedroom with another person. The size of homes ranged from 4 to 12 rooms, and the number of people in the home ranged from 3 to 10. Large families had both more people living in the home, $t(1,88.27$ [separate error terms]) $= -14.44$, $p < .001$, and more rooms in the home, $t(1,166) = -2.01$, $p < .05$, with large families having more rooms to accommodate the larger number of persons living in the home. These persons were by and large part of the nuclear rather than the extended family. Five families had a grandparent (all grandmothers) and one family had an uncle and another an aunt living with them. Small and large families did not differ in the number of adults in the home. Overall, children in this study had considerable household space.

With respect to *ethnicity* of the sample studied, mothers reported that 165 (98%) of the children in the study were white. One hundred sixty-one (96%) of the fathers in the study described themselves as white (four described themselves as Chicano, one as Asian, one as Indian, and one as black). One hundred sixty-two (96%) of the mothers described themselves as white (four described themselves as Chicano, one as Asian, and one as black).

Finally, these contextual factors used to describe the sample were compared across the three communities to determine the relevance of considering community differences in relation to sources of support. Of the 12 factors considered (father's age, mother's age, total population density, child density, older adult density, years living at present address, years living in present county, SES, number of cars owned, mother's employment status, number of rooms in home, and number of persons in household), six of these factors differentiated one community from the other two. Appendix A presents the F values, means, and standard deviations by community of those factors that did differ across community. Post hoc comparisons were made using the Tukey procedure, and in order to increase the homogeneity of the variances used in these contrasts, a square root transformation was also used for the population-density factors. The sample in Community U enjoyed higher SES and more rooms in their homes than was true for the sample from Community CS or Community R. Both Community U and Community CS experienced greater total population density than was true in Community R. Families in Community CS had lived longer in this same county than had the families in the other two communities. Community CS also offered greater child density than did the Community R. And finally, families in the rural sector owned more cars than families in town settings.

In sum, children interviewed in this study were growing up in relatively secure and low-stress conditions in modern American society. The children in this study had continuous contact with both parents and with at least one older sibling. The parents were young adults presumably ready for the demands of parenting (not "high-risk" teenage parents) at the time of the children's births. All fathers but one were employed, and 65% of the mothers were employed. No child was living in poverty conditions, and each child benefited from some degree of advantageous conditions afforded in American society by some minimal SES, comfortable housing conditions, and majority ethnic status. Finally, although there are some community differences, these children were living in what has traditionally been considered ideal, stable, small-town or rural conditions with parents having easy access to local community resources as well as the riches of major metropolitan centers (Campbell, 1981).

PROCEDURE

Children were identified through public birth records as well as enrollment records of churches, public and private schools, and child-oriented organizations such as 4-H and Girl Scouts or Boy Scouts. Parents of children were first contacted by phone to confirm sibling spacing and family size and to receive permission formally to invite the family to participate in a university-sponsored research project. Each family who did participate contributed about 7–8 hours (four home visits) with an interviewer in the first year of participation in an ongoing longitudinal program of research. Two-thirds (67%) of the families requested to participate did so. Our requirement of father participation in another aspect of this ongoing program of research seemed to contribute considerably to this "one-third" of nonparticipating families, as it was our impression that fathers were more likely than mothers or siblings to decline the opportunity to participate in this child development study. Fathers as a group were certainly more difficult to schedule interview sessions with than were mothers (even mothers working outside the home), older siblings, or the target children themselves.

The target child in each family was initially taken on a Neighborhood Walk to assess personal, home, and neighborhood/community resources.[1]

---

[1] It should be noted that the data from these 168 families were collected primarily in the summers of 1977, 1978, and 1979. During this time public services in California were

The actual walking around the neighborhood was intended both to elicit cues and reminders so as to encourage accurate and inclusive responding from children and to provide the children we interviewed with an activity (walking, guiding, pointing) in conjunction with an interview. Indeed, we were asking children in a most concrete manner to introduce us to their social and personal world as they knew and used it. Although we of course interviewed some shy children, the walks took us down manicured streets as well as into favorite fields or orchards (e.g., almond groves), empty lots, and favorite hiding places. Although children were frequently asked follow-up questions to document the accuracy of a previous answer, the interviews generally paced themselves into what felt like, to the interviewers, comfortable exposés of neighborhood life. Children did not appear to respond to the Neighborhood Walk as though it were a test; they did not ask how their answers compared to those given by other children.

The emphasis and perspective of this Neighborhood Walk were the child's reported experience of involvement with personal, home, and community resources. While some questions, such as, "Are there adults there

---

affected by Proposition 13. A brief assessment, independent of the children's report, was made in the county from which most of the children in this study were drawn and from one town with the most accessible school district and town records. What was found was that the county eliminated funding of the position of children's librarian. The county libraries offered no summer reading program in 1978, but then in 1979 a minimum reading program was established involving volunteer assistants. Library hours were cut from 30% to 60%, and book budgets were cut 27%, despite a 10% inflation figure. The 4-H programs took a 20% cut in overall budget, and this resulted in cuts in personnel such that programs continued to function but did do with less support from the main office of the program. Park and recreation programs were affected as well in two ways. The year-round after-school program was eliminated, and the financial charge for use of facilities (e.g., pool) was increased. Despite the increased fees, no enrollment change was noticed. The school programs were affected as well in at least four ways: there were fewer paid teachers' aides; summer school was eliminated in 1978 and reinstated on a tuition basis in 1979, but with enrollment substantially less than in years prior to 1978; the all-district art program was cut; and the all-district music program was eliminated in the elementary schools and then reinstated in January 1980, as a tuition program (enrollment figures in this tuition program are as high as pretuition figures were). In addition, a number of non-state-funded programs were unaffected by Proposition 13. Little League, Girl Scouts, Boy Scouts, and a private art center are examples of such organizations. By and large, the changes reflect issues of quality of programs more than quantity and accessibility of programs to children in this particular county. To assess the impact of Proposition 13 on children's reporting of their involvement in formally sponsored organizations, a comparison was made of involvement in structured and unstructured formally sponsored organizations and of accessibility of these organizations by year of participation in the study. No significant differences according to year of participation, that is, no cohort effects, were found. This highlights the fact that the Neighborhood Walk assesses not the quality of formally sponsored organizations but rather the extent of participation in such organizations as reported by the children.

you have special talks with?" and "Whom would you go to if you were sad and wanted someone to talk to?" reflect a quality of intimacy with certain individuals, the majority of the questions reflect concern about the existence (or quantity) and extent of sources of support. This Neighborhood Walk does not assess why children do or do not report experiencing particular sources of support. It does not assess whether, for example, if a child does not report using a library, it is because there is no library available to the child to use. Similarly, this interview does not assess why a child does not report visiting grandparents. Some grandparents not visited are undoubtedly not alive; others may well live quite far away. This Neighborhood Walk emphasizes the child's experience of sources of support and does not investigate the reasons for the absence of such support. The Neighborhood Walk interview is fairly structured, containing frequent follow-up questions designed to tap thoughtful responses. For example, names and dates are frequently elicited not as information to be scored but as a means to increase thoughtful, valid responses. With this in mind, Appendix B provides the interviewer protocol of the Neighborhood Walk used in the present study. Scoring of the Neighborhood Walk will be thoroughly described in a later chapter.

While children were going on their Neighborhood Walk, their mothers provided the basic demographic information used above in describing the sample. Following the Neighborhood Walk, an array of measures assessing how children experience themselves and others in social situations (i.e., social-emotional functioning) were administered. These will be thoroughly discussed in the next chapter.

IV. MEASUREMENT OF SOCIAL-EMOTIONAL FUNCTIONING IN MIDDLE CHILDHOOD

A series of measures designed to assess children's view of themselves and others in social situations was administered.[2] This included nine measures that were administered to both the 7- and the 10-year-old subjects in this study: (*a*) empathy (Bryant, 1982); (*b*) acceptance of individual differences (Bryant, 1982); (*c*) social perspective taking (Rothenberg, 1970); (*d*) locus of control (Nowicki & Duke, 1974; Nowicki & Strickland, 1973); attitudes about (*e*) cooperative, (*f*) competitive, and (*g*) individualistic working environments (Ahlgren, Christensen, & Lum, 1977); (*h*) acceptance of help (Maccoby, 1961); and (*i*) acceptance of self or general self-evaluation (Zingale, Edwards, & Yarvis, 1978). Two additional measures were developed for 10-year-old children: tolerance for ambivalence of feelings and tolerance for ambiguity in interpersonal situations. Appendix C summarizes measurement concerns for all these measures. With respect to scoring, a z score was computed for the locus of control measure since the scale for younger children consisted of 26 items, as compared to the 40 items in the form used with older children. Furthermore, a high score on the locus of control measure reflects a strong internal orientation. A low score on the acceptance of individual differences measure, however, presumably reflects strong acceptance of individual differences. For all other measures, high scores reflect strength of the attitude or skill reflected by the name of the measure.

These measures were selected or designed with the intent of measuring the child's status on attitudes and perceptions about issues of autonomy (e.g., locus of control; attitudes about individualistic working conditions) as well as issues of relatedness (e.g., acceptance of help, empathy, acceptance of individual differences in others). These dimensions were seen as conceptually important since they reflect what clinicians such as Erikson (1964) and

---

[2] Measurements of ego strength/hope (Gottschalk, 1974) and evaluation of handicapped child presented scoring difficulties and so were omitted from the present analysis.

Minuchin (1974) and researchers of childhood resilience such as Murphy (1974) and Werner and Smith (1982) view as the major developmental challenges for psychological and social well-being. Developing a sense of autonomy as well as developing a sense of relatedness represent primary developmental challenges for social-emotional resilience and well-being.

A second conceptual basis for measure selection was used. Aspects of instrumental as well as expressive competence were considered. Being able to take the perspective of another can be viewed as an instrumental activity since it can enable one to make use of this information to negotiate more skillfully with another. Empathic experiences and tolerance for ambivalence of feelings, on the other hand, may be viewed as expressive competence in that they reflect the quality or ability of one to experience a wide variety of feelings even though there is no material gain that is thereby accrued. Additionally, arguments have been made that being both instrumental and expressive is the basis for the richest expression of individual development that bypasses the traditional constraints of rigid sex-role definitions (Bem, 1975).

At the time this study was designed, only seven instruments were identified from the existing research literature that met these conceptual criteria, and relatively little data had been published on their measurement integrity. Locus of control, probably the most researched construct available, had a reported internal consistency of .63 and 6-week test-retest reliability of .63 for third, fourth, and fifth graders (Nowicki & Strickland, 1973) and a reported internal consistency of .79 for 7-year-olds (S. Nowicki & M. Duke, personal communication, 1973). The social perspective taking measure had a reported interrater reliability of .86–.96 and internal consistency of .28–.47 (Rothenberg, 1970). The measures of assessing attitudes toward cooperation, competition, and individualism had reported internal consistency of .72, .82, and .74, respectively (Ahlgren et al., 1977), although these figures were based on the responses of children spanning the school years. Neither the acceptance of help measure developed by Maccoby (1961) nor the self-evaluation measure developed by Zingale et al. (1978) had established reliability scores. The acceptance of help measure was conceptually of interest because of its intent to measure comfort with dependency, an aspect of interpersonal functioning too long neglected by researchers in our culture, which strongly values independence. Internal consistency scores for the present sample were .51 for the 7-year-olds and .40 for the 10-year-olds. The self-evaluation in relation to peers was designed to assess three different aspects of development: positive internal experiences, school performance, and social relations. Internal consistency for these three items considered together was .61 for the 7-year-olds and .42 for the 10-year-olds. With the exception of measures regarding attitudes toward cooperation, competition, and individualism in one context (an academic work setting), the internal consistency scores of these existing middle childhood measures of social-emotional functioning are low and may, at best, indicate the lower boundary for other forms of reliability and highlight the multidimensional nature of social-emotional functioning.

In response to the presumed multidimensional nature of social-emotional functioning, test-retest reliability was considered the most appropriate form of reliability to consider. Consequently, 2-week test-retest reliability was obtained for the measures being developed to assess tolerance for ambiguity, tolerance for ambivalence of feelings, acceptance of individual differences (Bryant, 1982), and empathy (Bryant, 1982). Reliability involving 7-year-olds was in the mid-.70s and ranged from .81 to .86 for the 10-year-olds. While existing validity data on these measures are reported in Appendix C, the lack of well-developed measures for assessing social-emotional functioning during middle childhood is a continuing problem for researchers in this area. Furthermore, our understanding of the nature of social-emotional functioning and traditional measurement standards often conflict (Bryant, 1984). Rather than dismiss research in this area of middle childhood functioning, continuing work on scale development and relevant measurement standards is required. Meanwhile, caution is needed when interpreting lack of association among existing measures of ill-defined reliability. In the present study, a procedure was used to reduce the number of "outcome" measures used to assess the value of support in predicting social-emotional functioning during middle childhood and, in part, to limit the overuse of measures that require cautious interpretation.

Appendix D presents the means, standard deviations, and obtained ranges of scores found for the measures of social-emotional functioning considered in this study.

To consider the possible overlap among the various measures, data from each age group were submitted to a principal component factor analysis with varimax rotation. The factor analysis of the data obtained from 10-year-olds yielded four factors with eigenvalues greater than one. The four factors were labeled *perspective taking orientation, attitudes toward interpersonal relatedness, sharing vulnerable feelings with others,* and *acceptance of self and others.* Perspective taking orientation included social perspective taking skill (Rothenberg, 1970), locus of control orientation (Nowicki & Strickland, 1973), tolerance for ambivalence of feelings (App. C), and tolerance for ambiguity in interpersonal situations (App. C). Each of these four measures presents the child with interpersonal situations that require interpretation of the feelings and/or motives of self or others; that is, the child is required to take the perspective of self and others in order to interpret a variety of social situations. Attitudes toward interpersonal relatedness included attitudes toward competition, cooperation, and individualistic working environments in school settings (Ahlgren et al., 1977). Of note is that, among 10-

TABLE 1

Principal Factor Analysis (Varimax Rotation) of Measures of Psychological
Well-Being for 10-Year-Olds

Measures	Factor 1	Factor 2	Factor 3	Factor 4
Social perspective taking	.71[a]	−.01	.06	.11
Tolerance for ambiguity	.54[a]	−.15	−.21	−.10
Locus of control	.48[a]	.00	−.06	.26
Tolerance for ambivalence	.47[a]	.02	.13	.02
Attitudes toward competition	−.07	.70[a]	.21	.00
Attitudes toward cooperation	−.15	−.63[a]	.16	.09
Attitudes toward individualism	−.11	.47[a]	.04	−.08
Empathy	.37	−.32	.57[a]	−.04
Acceptance of help	−.09	.17	.45[a]	−.00
Self-evaluation	.04	−.04	−.15	.56[a]
Acceptance of individual differences	−.09	.11	−.22	−.46[a,b]

[a] Loadings ≥ .45. Measures with these loadings were used in defining each factor.
[b] A low score indicates great acceptance of individual differences.

year-olds, great enjoyment of competition and individualism is associated with little enjoyment of cooperation and vice versa. Whereas Johnson and Norem-Hebeisen (1979) found that attitudes toward competition and cooperation are independent of each other among 17- and 18-year-olds (i.e., twelfth graders), this is apparently not the case among these 10-year-olds. Sharing vulnerable feelings with others included reported empathy with the feelings of others (Bryant, 1982) and willingness to accept help from others (Maccoby, 1961); and acceptance of self and others included acceptance of individual differences (Bryant, 1982) and acceptance of self or general self-evaluation (Zingale et al., 1978). Table 1 presents the results of this factor analysis. Noteworthy is the clarity of these factors with individual measures each loading relatively strongly (loading value ≥ .45) on only one factor.

While the factor analysis of the 11 measures using the data from 10-year-olds yielded four principal factors, each primarily based on two or more measures and exhausting all 11 measures, the intercorrelation matrix of the nine measures given to the younger age group could not be similarly reduced. Table 2 presents the results of this latter factor analysis of the data obtained from 7-year-olds. In this analysis, each of the four factors having eigenvalues greater than one were defined by one and only one measure. The extracted factors for the first graders in essence merely repeated the variable list.

Evidently, unlike the 10-year-olds, among the 7-year-olds the nine measures were not correlated in any meaningful fashion. Barring the possibility that these results reflect lowered reliability of measures among the 7-year-olds, it appears that the younger children have not yet developed the inte-

TABLE 2

PRINCIPAL FACTOR ANALYSIS (Varimax Rotation) OF MEASURES OF PSYCHOLOGICAL
WELL-BEING FOR 7-YEAR-OLDS

Measures	Factor 1	Factor 2	Factor 3	Factor 4
Social perspective taking	.10	.06	−.10	.26
Locus of control	.92[a]	.02	.07	.13
Attitudes toward competition	.14	.07	.82[a]	−.02
Attitudes toward cooperation	.11	−.08	.10	.35
Attitudes toward individualism	.10	.93[a]	.20	−.11
Empathy	−.10	−.11	.01	.53[a]
Acceptance of help	−.11	.22	.17	.33
Self-evaluation	.14	−.05	−.24	−.06
Acceptance of individual differences	.31	.25	−.12	−.01[a,b]

[a] Loadings ≥ .45.
[b] A low score indicates great acceptance of individual differences.

gration required for more complex underlying response or habit clusters characterizing the 10-year-old sample.

These findings have theoretical implications for our understanding of development during middle childhood. The findings are congruent with Werner's (1948) theoretical perspective that development is multilinear rather than linear. As Langer describes Werner's theory, several "selves," individuated systems of action, develop initially side by side: "The mark of normal development is that these differentiated 'selves' are progressively related into a functionally and structurally hierarchized organizational whole in which the constituent parts are not lost but integrated" (1969, p. 92). Lewin also considers hierarchical organization to increase with age and to be a primary characteristic of developmental processes. The differential factor structures generated by the 7- and 10-year-olds in this study support these views of development.

Additionally, traditional psychoanalytic theory labels middle childhood as a period of latency with respect to significant personality development (Freud, 1953), a position that has apparently discouraged the empirical research of personality and social development during middle childhood (Lamb, 1978; Scarr, 1979). But the present findings are congruent with the theoretical perspective of Sullivan (1953), who argues that middle childhood is a period of active development involving integration of social and affective phenomena. Seven-year-old children who are at the beginning phase of middle childhood apparently do not experience social and affective phenomenon with the same coherence or integration as do children in a later phase of middle childhood (10-year-olds). Such findings may help create a developmental perspective on our understanding of personality development during middle childhood that will reveal middle childhood to be a period of developmental significance. These findings also signal for us that the expression of social and affective development may well not be related to contextual variables in the same way for the 7-year-olds as for the 10-year-olds.

Finally, the factor analyses provided the basis for selecting a reduced number of dependent (outcome) variables of social-emotional functioning to consider in relation to sources of support identified in the Neighborhood Walk. One measure from each factor of both the first- and the fourth-grade factor analyses was selected. With this criterion, the following six measures will be considered in subsequent analyses: empathy, acceptance of individual differences, attitudes toward competition, social perspective taking, locus of control, and attitudes toward individualism. This reduction of the number of measures of social-emotional functioning for subsequent data analyses represents an attempt to reduce the likelihood of spurious findings caused by collinearity. Since for the 10-year-olds both locus of control and social perspective taking load strongly on the first factor and attitudes toward both competition and individualism load strongly on the second factor, care will be taken to avoid overinterpretation of results that merely reflect collinearity of measures with strong loadings on the same factor for the older children in this study. Choosing measures that reflect the factor structures of both age groups, however, offers greater assurance that the dependent measures of social-emotional functioning considered in this study are meaningful to both age groups studied.

V. SOURCES OF SUPPORT DERIVED FROM THE NEIGHBORHOOD WALK

CONCEPTUAL FRAMEWORK FOR SCORING THE NEIGHBORHOOD WALK

Support is an elusive construct. Walker, MacBride, and Vachon (1977) have identified four possible aspects or kinds of support: maintenance of social identity; emotional support, including facilitation of feelings of being understood and cared for; material aid and services; and information and access to new or broader knowledge. Sources of support are viewed as persons, places, and/or activities that serve to provide opportunities with affective and/or material meaning. This definition encompasses aspects of individual autonomy as intrapersonal sources of support, relatedness to others by measurement of social support network variables, and environmental factors that foster the availability of sources of support. With respect to definition of social support, this study favors the inclusion of family members in the child's household (Lewis & Weinraub, 1976), and this precludes the more restrictive definition of Cochran and Brassard (1979), who do not include family members in one's household. Indeed, it is the author's view that a child's "family" of meaningful, developmentally significant individuals may include individuals not formally recognized as belonging to the child's circle of household relatives. It is here that a child-focused perspective can aid our understanding of this matter. With respect to social support (i.e., others as support), the scoring procedures developed for the Neighborhood Walk are congruent with the scoring procedures reported by Blyth et al. (1982), which use an unlimited number of particular kinds of relations, and by Garbarino et al. (1978), which use the top ten significant others. Overall, the scoring procedures of the Neighborhood Walk considered structural qualities of the child's support system such as size, homogeneity, and accessibility as well as functional/interactional qualities such as frequency and degree of involvement (i.e., casual versus intimate relationship).

Three major aspects of reported support in this study using the Neighborhood Walk were considered: others as resources (primarily interpersonal in nature), intrapersonal sources of support, and environmental sources of support. Casual, intimate, and categorically important relations form the basis for distinguishing kinds of relationships when considering others as sources of support. An outline of categories representing sources of support derived from the Neighborhood Walk follows.

    I. Others as resources (primarily interpersonal sources of support)
       A. Peer generation
          1. Know and interact with peers
          2. Intimate talks with peers
          3. Peer generation among the 10 most important individuals
       B. Pet "generation"
          1. Pets as special friends
          2. Intimate talks with pets
          3. Pet "generation" among the 10 most important individuals
       C. Parent generation
          1. Know and interact with adult generation
          2. Special talks with adults
          3. Intimate talks with parent generation
          4. Parent generation among the 10 most important individuals
          5. Involvement in father's work
          6. Involvement in mother's work
       D. Grandparent generation
          1. Know and interact with grandparent generation
          2. Intimate talks with grandparent generation
          3. Grandparent generation among the 10 most important individuals
       E. Spiritual support[3]
   II. Intrapersonal sources of support
       A. Hobbies
       B. Fantasies
          1. Structured
          2. Unstructured
       C. Access to skill development and public display of skills
 III. Environmental sources of support
       A. Access to independence (places to get off to by self)
       B. Places to join others

---

[3] Scores for references to God as a source of support resulted in an extremely skewed distribution with enormous kurtosis so that this category of support was not available for statistical analysis.

1. Formally sponsored organizations
   a. Structured
   b. Unstructured
2. Informal, unsponsored meeting places

These 23 Neighborhood Walk support categories and their operational definitions are presented in Appendix E, and the means, standard deviations, and obtained ranges of these support variables are presented in Appendix F.[4] Additional categories of support included elaborated considerations of accessibility. These will be presented in Chapter VII.

RELIABILITY

Two-week interval, test-retest reliability of these categories was established on a sample of 19 7- and 10-year-olds and, with two noted exceptions, was quite high. With the exception of two of the 23 categories, structured fantasy and pets among the 10 most important individuals, the test-retest Pearson product-moment correlations ranged from .85 to 1.00. In fact, 70% of these reliability coefficients were in the .90s. Overall, the stability of children's responses was remarkably strong.

Consistent with the findings of Vaillancourt (1973), the question in the Neighborhood Walk requiring a value judgment (i.e., top ten individuals) elicited less stable responses. Identifying pets as among the 10 most important individuals, $r(17) = .69$, was the least stable of these top 10 categories. Not only did the top ten questions require value judgments, but they also arbitrarily limited the number of most important individuals, a factor that could in part contribute to indecision and lowered reliability for these particular categories. That the top ten question itself is a challenge to reliability is further supported by the strong reliability scores of the other scores involving pets, ranging from .92 for intimate talks with pet generation to .99 for pets as special friends. One exception to the relatively lower reliability of top ten categories involved grandparent generation members in the top ten lists, $r(17) = .98$. Apparently, there is little ambiguity in children's judgments regarding the importance of the grandparent generation in their lives.

The second category with low reliability involved the reporting of structured fantasies, $r(17) = .57$. The low reliability of this category was apparently due to an actual change in a child's life rather than to poor reporting. During the 2-week interval between interview sessions, a child had acquired

[4] An initial categorization according to sex, relative age of peer (younger, same age, or older), and familial relationship (immediate relative, extended relative, or nonrelative) indicated many categories with problematic distributions, that is, distributions with skewness scores greater than 2 and kurtosis scores greater than 6. Thus refined analysis according to relative age of peer as well as sex and familial status was abandoned.

a television for her bedroom, and in reality the amount of television viewing did likely increase dramatically. In another family, a grandparent died during the 2-week interval, and some changes in scores resulted for this child as well. In other words, sources of support can be added or withdrawn over a relatively short period of time. Overall, though, the generally high reliability obtained suggests a fairly high degree of stability in support conditions as reported by children.

Percent agreement was also calculated as an additional measure of reliability. More specifically, the percentage of test and retest scores that were the same or that differed only by 1 point was calculated. With the exception of one category, skill development and expression, these agreements ranged between 84% and 100%. In fact, 74% of these reliability scores were in the 90s (or 100%). In the case of skill development, for which the range of scores was greatest (2–20), only one child differed by 3 points, and none by more than that. The Pearson product-moment correlation for this category was .97. Percent agreement scores indicate notable stability of responses.

In sum, according to both measures of reliability (i.e., Pearson product-moment correlations and percent agreement scores), the stability of children's responses about sources of support in their lives was strong.

DEVELOPMENTAL AND FAMILIAL CONTEXT IN RELATION TO REPORTED SUPPORT

To obtain a better understanding of how perceived support is related to developmental and family contextual variables, multivariate analyses were utilized. More specifically, three MANOCOVAs were completed to consider the possible effects of sex, age, family size, and sex of sibling in addition to all possible two-way and three-way interactions of these factors in relation to children's reporting of others as sources of support, intrapersonal sources of support, and environmental sources of support; and SES was included as a covariate to assess the possible confounding of family size or age effects with SES of the family. Univariate ANOVAs were then computed to explain further these three factors that were significant in the MANOCOVA results. When two- and three-way interactions were involved, Newman-Keuls procedures for contrasts were used.

Others as Sources of Support

The first MANOCOVA, based on the 15 "interpersonal" support categories, yielded three significant main effects: sex of target child, $F(12,140)$ = 2.78, $p < .01$; age of target child, $F(12,140)$ = 1.98, $p < .05$; and family size, $F(15,149)$ = 2.49, $p < .01$. All MANOCOVA F values represent multivariate approximate F's. There were no interaction effects.

With respect to sex differences, males more than females know and interact with the adult generation, $F(1,151) = 6.32$, $p < .01$, and tended to do the same with the peer generation, $F(1,151) = 3.13$, $p < .08$, while females, more than males, report more intimate talks with peers, $F(1,151) = 8.79$, $p < .01$, and tended to do the same with both the parent generation, $F(1,151) = 3.08$, $p < .09$, and with pets, $F(1,151) = 2.85$, $p < .10$, and to have pets as special friends, $F(1,151) = 4.04$, $p < .05$. These findings support those reported in the literature that males seek out more extensive relationships than females, whereas females seek out fewer but more intensive relationships (Berndt, 1981; Waldrop & Halverson, 1975). While the males in this study reported knowing and interacting with more adults in their neighborhoods than did females, the males did not report more intimate talks with the adult generation than did females. Females did report more intimate interactions with peers than did their male counterparts.

With respect to family size, children from small families, as compared with children from large families, tended to report more intimate talks with the parent generation, $F(1,151) = 3.66$, $p < .06$, while children from large families, more than children from small families, tended to report that they know and interact more with peers, $F(1,151) = 6.89$, $p < .01$, have more peers among the 10 most important individuals in their lives, $F(1,151) = 6.18$, $p < .02$, and have more intimate talks with the grandparent generation, $F(1,151) = 4.26$, $p < .05$. Although the differences according to family size are not pervasive, the results do suggest that children in small families are more intimately involved with their parents than are children in large families. This coincides with Bossard and Boll's (1956) formulation that parents in large families, by distributing their time and energy among the various family members, are not as likely to require or engage as strong an emotional interaction with any one child as is true of parents with a small number of children. Additionally, it appears that children in large families find others among their peer and grandparent generations and the neighborhood pet population to compensate perhaps for the less intense involvment with their parents. Regardless, it does appear, as White (1976) has argued, that to some extent the large family and the very small family yield different worlds to the developing child.

With respect to age differences, 7-year-olds, as compared to 10-year-olds, reported more peers to be among the 10 most important individuals in their lives, $F(1,151) = 4.41$, $p < .05$, while 10-year-olds tended to report more intimate talks with the grandparent generation, $F(1,151) = 3.62$, $p < .06$, and reported more parent- and grandparent-generation persons as among the 10 most important individuals in their lives than did their younger counterparts, $F(1,151) = 4.44$, $p < .05$, and $F(1,151) = 3.84$, $p < .05$, respectively. Ten-year-olds also reported more pets as special friends, $F(1,151) = 6.67$, $p < .05$, and greater involvement in their father's work,

$F(1,151) = 4.89$, $p < .05$. Overall, 10-year-olds appear to have more elaborated sources of support. The findings that 7-year-olds find more peers to be among the most important individuals in their lives may reflect this less elaborated network of sources of support. Regardless, these findings suggest caution in overgeneralizing the popular notion that, with age, children increasingly turn to their peer group for support.

Intrapersonal Sources of Support

The second MANOCOVA, based on the four intrapersonal support measures, yielded two main effects: sex of the target child, $F(4,148) = 2.54$, $p < .05$, and age of the target child, $F(4,148) = 8.70$, $p < .001$. One three-way interaction was significant—sex of target child × family size × sex of older sibling, $F(4,148) = 4.29$, $p < .01$. In the univariate follow-ups, this three-way interaction held for structured fantasies, $F(1,151) = 13.15$, $p < .001$. Not only do girls tend to report greater use of structured fantasies than do boys, but girls with an older sister in large families ($M = 6.43$, SD = 4.42) report greater use of structured fantasies than do girls with an older sister in small families ($M = 3.62$, SD = 4.24), boys with an older sister in large families ($M = 3.38$, SD = 2.20), and boys with an older brother in small families ($M = 3.10$, SD = 2.23).

With respect to sex differences, then, females report greater use of internal support strategies than do males. This held true as a trend for both structured fantasies, $F(1,151) = 3.05$, $p < .09$, and hobbies, $F(1,151) = 3.56$, $p < .07$. This sex effect, coupled with both a particular influence of an older sister with presumably a similar predisposition toward relatively high use of structured fantasy and the context of a large family in which, in comparison to small families, children are more likely to turn to peers, may account for the greatest use of structured fantasy reported by girls with an older sister in large families.

With respect to age differences, the older children in this study report greater involvement in skill development and expression, $F(1,151) = 32.60$, $p < .001$. With age, then, it appears that, in at least one respect, children gain sources of intrapersonal support.

Environmental Sources of Support

The last MANOCOVA, based on the four environmental support measures, yielded one main effect, age of target child, $F(4,148) = 4.81$, $p < .001$, and one two-way interaction, age × sex of target child, $F(4,148) = 2.59$, $p < .05$.

Older children tended to have more places to get off to by themselves, $F(1,151) = 3.34$, $p < .08$. Types of places children reported using to get off to by themselves were categorized into the following eight groups: own room, in house (but not own room), outside in yard, in a vehicle, in a neighborhood location, garage, relative's home, and nonrelative's home. Only the reporting of using one's own room as a place to get off to by oneself was clearly different for the 7- and 10-year-olds. Seventy-seven percent of the 10-year-olds, compared with only 49% of the 7-year-olds, reported their own room as a place they used to get off to by themselves. This suggests a greater interest in privacy among the older children rather than greater freedom per se to locate privacy.

Older children also have or make greater use of opportunities for both skill development and expression, $F(1,151) = 32.90, p < .001$, and formally sponsored organizations with structured activities, $F(1,151) = 16.68, p < .001$, than do younger children. Furthermore, males, in particular, make greater use, with age, of these formally sponsored organizations with structured activities, $F(1,151) = 8.37, p < .01$. Whether older children, and boys in particular, seek out these experiences and/or are encouraged to do so by the parents or others remains undetermined.

ILLUSTRATIONS OF RANGE OF CONTENT WITHIN SUPPORT CATEGORIES

Within the categories of support presented thus far, there can be considerable variation as to the specific form that support can take. In an effort to consider various general types of support across children in the study, the specific form within a support category was lost in the scoring procedures.

To be better aware of this "hidden" richness of support, three illustrations of the range of form within a support factor, one interpersonal support factor, one intrapersonal support issue, and one environmental support issue will be presented.

Ten Most Important Individuals

Since there is existing research on children's (adolescents') report of important individuals in their lives (Blyth et al., 1982; Garbarino et al., 1978), the content of this area of interpersonal support will be considered. This descriptive analysis takes into account both the generation and the relative versus nonrelative status of the important individuals. Table 3 presents the percentages of children (broken down by age of child) who reported these classifications of persons as the 10 most important individuals in their lives. While 80% of the sample identified their mothers and 79% identified their fathers as among the 10 most important individuals, aunts, uncles, and grandparents as well as nonrelative adults were clearly important to children in this study. Twenty-three percent identified at least one nonrelative adult in their top ten list. This is roughly consistent with the 26% of the adolescents' who reported extended family and nonrelated adults in

TABLE 3

Percentages of Relatives and Nonrelatives among 10 Most Important Individuals

Who Is Important	Peer Generation			Parent Generation			Grandparent Generation			Adult Generation[a]		
	7-Year-Olds (N = 72)	10-Year-Olds (N = 96)	Total (N = 168)	7-Year-Olds (N = 72)	10-Year-Olds (N = 96)	Total (N = 168)	7-Year-Olds (N = 72)	10-Year-Olds (N = 96)	Total (N = 168)	7-Year-Olds (N = 72)	10-Year-Olds (N = 96)	Total (N = 168)
Relatives:												
At least one	86	84	85	90	96	94	39	52	46	94	96	95
At least two	47	48	48	88	96	92	35	47	42	92	96	94
At least three	21	26	24	24	35	30	17	24	21	51	64	58
Nonrelatives:												
At least one	72	72	72	22	22	22	0	2	1	22	23	23
At least two	63	53	57	14	14	14	0	2	1	14	14	14
At least three	53	40	45	7	7	7	0	1	60	7	7	8
Relatives or nonrelatives:												
At least one	94	95	95	93	96	95	39	55	48	94	96	95
At least two	88	77	82	89	96	93	35	50	44	90	96	94
At least three ...	79	62	69	36	54	46	17	25	21	57	72	66

[a] Adult generation = parent generation + grandparent generation.

Blyth et al.'s (1982) study and the 22% for a comparable group in Garbarino et al.'s (1978) study.

Overall, it is remarkable that a majority of the children, without being prompted to do so, included at least three peer generation members and at least three adult generation members in their top ten lists. It appears considerably easier (at least more frequent) for children to garner important peer relationships among those who are nonrelatives than it is for them to do so among both the parent and the grandparent generations. When adult generation is broken down into parent versus grandparent generation, it is clear that these children are especially limited in the extent to which grandparent-generation members are involved in these top ten ratings. Age-segregation factors, including life-span limitations as well as housing factors separating children from older adults, may be operating to effect this limited reporting of the grandparent generation in the top ten.

With respect to the importance of siblings, 80% of the children listed at least one sibling in their top ten. This appears to be somewhat less than the 90% of adolescents reported to have done so by Blyth et al. (1982). Although there were differences in method, one could cautiously consider that siblings become somewhat more important in adolescence than they are in middle childhood. Nonetheless, 76% of the children in this study included all their siblings in their top ten.

Table 4 presents the actual percentages of siblings among the 10 most important individuals according to the child's family size. What is not shown in this table is the perceived importance of the target older sibling identified as 2–3 years older than the target child interviewed in this study. Eighty-four percent of these target older siblings were identified among the top ten. This 84% held for the target older siblings of both 7-year-olds and 10-year-olds. More target older sisters (95%) than older brothers (73%) were identified in the top ten, $\chi^2(1) = 13.15$, $p < .001$. In fact, these target older sisters showed the highest percentage of representation on these top ten lists, higher than that of mothers or fathers. From the child's perspective,

TABLE 4

PERCENTAGES OF SIBLINGS AMONG 10 MOST IMPORTANT INDIVIDUALS BY FAMILY SIZE

Family Size	7-Year-Olds	10-Year-Olds	Total
Small families (N)	36	48	84
Their one sibling (%)	78	79	79
Large families (N)	36	48	84
At least one sibling (%)	86	79	82
At least two siblings (%)	78	69	73
All siblings (%)	69	60	68
All families (N)	72	96	168
At least one sibling (%)	82	79	80
All siblings (%)	74	70	76

then, siblings are very important individuals in their lives, and older sisters in particular merit our regard.

Places to Get Off to by Oneself

Ninety-two percent of the children had at least one place to get off to by themselves. Only 21% had at least two such places. The places children seek out to be alone, in order of percentage used by children who had at least one place for privacy, are own room (70%); outside in yard (20%); in a neighborhood location (19%); in house, not including own room (4%); in a vehicle (2%); in the garage (2%); at a relative's home (1%); and at a nonrelative's home (1%). These children predominantly make use of their own room. This was especially true for the older children in this sample, $\chi^2(1) = 9.93$, $p < .01$. Furthermore, sharing a room did not necessarily preclude experiences of privacy there. Forty-five percent of the children who shared a bedroom reported using their bedroom as a place to be alone. Other places may be peopled at times but available for experiences of aloneness also. These places were frequently categorized as in a neighborhood location: park, alley, streets (for bicycle riding), church, clubhouse, and orchard. Overall, consider that almost all the children reported at least one place to get off to by themselves, that children reported an average of two places they used to experience aloneness, that children reliably reported using such places, and that children reported a rich variety of locations in which they could have solitary experience. These facts suggest that the opportunity for aloneness is a salient experience in children's lives and warrants more elaborated consideration in developmental research.

PLACES TO WHICH CHILDREN FANTASIZE RUNNING OFF

Seven-year-olds (49%) were more likely than were 10-year-olds (28%) to report having a place they fantasize about running off to, $\chi^2(1) = 5.83$, $p < .03$. As indicated by the percentages in Table 5, no single kind of place was a majority representative of these "pretend places." In other words, although the fantasies about running away were more frequent among the younger children in this study, the specific form of these fantasies remained fairly idiosyncratic. It should be noted, however, that running away did not necessarily involve being alone. The issue of autonomy represented by this category involves autonomy from one's immediate family but may or may not involve relatedness to others outside the child's home.

THE NEIGHBORHOOD AS A PSYCHOLOGICAL PHENOMENON

Finally, to consider the extent to which the Neighborhood Walk represented a psychological phenomenon as opposed to a collective, sociological

TABLE 5

PERCENTAGE USE OF PARTICULAR KINDS OF PLACES FANTASIZED
ABOUT "RUNNING OFF TO"

Place	7-Year-Olds ($N = 35$)	10-Year-Olds ($N = 28$)	Total ($N = 63$)
Neighborhood—private areas	31	25	30
Neighborhood—public areas	14	0	8
Country, nature	3	11	6
Friends in town	6	7	6
Relatives in town	6	4	5
Out-of-town, United States	3	11	6
Out-of-town relatives	0	7	3
Other countries	6	18	11
Playland (e.g., Disneyland)	14	0	8
Otherworldly (e.g., religious)	3	0	2
Restaurants, stores	9	0	5
Imaginary play	6	4	5
Outer space	0	4	2

NOTE.—N is the number of children who fantasized about running away.

phenomenon, correlations based on the responses of 33 pairs of children drawn from the same census track were compared, using z score procedures, with correlations based on the responses of 35 pairs of children from the same community but a different census tract. Of the 23 support-category comparisons, only two (grandparents in top ten and knowing and interacting with peers) were significant ($p < .05$). In both instances, the correlations in the same and a different census tract are opposite to what one would expect in a collective analysis; the scores were inversely related for children in the same census tract but positively related for children in different census tracts. Overall, these results attest to the individual, psychological nature of the conceptualization and scoring of this Neighborhood Walk procedure.

SUMMARY

Three major aspects of support were considered: others as resources (primarily interpersonal in nature), intrapersonal sources of support, and environmental sources of support. Using the Neighborhood Walk procedure of interviewing and scoring provides a reasonably reliable (often quite reliable) avenue for children in middle childhood to speak for themselves. The extent to which children experience these three kinds of support is related to developmental (e.g., age and sex of child) and family context (e.g., family size) factors as well as to the specific form that support variables take.

VI. PREDICTING SOCIAL-EMOTIONAL FUNCTIONING

While the reliability and use of support categories derived from the Neighborhood Walk have been discussed, the validity of these child reports can in part be determined by considering their usefulness in predicting social-emotional functioning. Predicting social-emotional functioning is, therefore, the focus of this chapter. The predictive value of developmental factors (e.g., age and sex of child), family context (e.g., family size), and sources of support was considered with respect to social-emotional functioning (i.e., empathy, acceptance of individual differences in others, attitudes toward competition, attitudes toward individualism, social perspective taking skill, and locus of control). Finally, sex of sibling and SES were considered as controls so as not to misinterpret the role of the family context as a moderating factor.

First a MANOCOVA was completed to consider the possible effects of sex of the child, age of the child, family size, and sex of older sibling in addition to all possible two-way and three-way interactions of these factors in relation to children's scores on the selected measures of social-emotional functioning, and SES was included as a covariate. This MANOCOVA yielded a significant sex of child effect, $F(4,146) = 4.38, p < .01$, an age of child effect, $F(4,146) = 22.89, p < .001$, and an age $\times$ sex of child interaction, $F(4,146) = 2.20, p < .05$.

Subsequent univariate analyses of variances with SES used as a covariate were made on individual outcome measures to assess these effects. With the exception of attitudes toward individualism and locus of control orientation, the selected measures of social-emotional functioning appeared sensitive to age or sex of child respondent. Empathy revealed an age effect, $F(1,151) = 5.04, p < .05$, with the 10-year-olds expressing greater empathy than the 7-year-olds, and a sex of respondent effect, $F(1,151) = 15.46, p < .001$, with females expressing greater empathy than males. The acceptance of individual difference measure revealed an age effect, $F(1,151) = 4.60, p < .05$, with the 10-year-olds expressing greater acceptance of individuals than the 7-

year-olds, and a sex of respondent effect, $F(1,151) = 4.00, p < .05$, with females expressing greater acceptance of individual differences among peers than males. Attitudes toward competition revealed a sex effect, $F(1,151) = 5.43, p < .05$, with males expressing greater competitiveness than females, and an age × sex of respondent interaction, $F(1,151) = 8.72, p < .01$. Ten-year-old boys were more competitive than were 7-year-old boys, $F(1,164) = 6.85, p < .001$. Girls at the two ages did not differ from each other on competitive attitudes. Whereas 7-year-old boys and girls did not differ in their attitudes toward competition, 10-year-old boys were more competitive than girls of the same age, $F(1,164) = 7.50, p < .001$. Figure 2 illustrates this interaction. Social-affective perspective taking revealed a large age effect, $F(1,151) = 125.72, p < .001$, with 10-year-olds more skilled at social perspective taking than 7-year-olds.

So that these effects can be understood better, Appendix G presents the means and standard deviations broken down by age and sex for measures that were sensitive to these dimensions.

To consider the value of the children's reported sources of support, the 23 support variables described in the previous section were organized into seven sets and were initially considered as predictor variables. To assess the potential for redundancy and collinearity among variables within these conceptually derived support sets as well as confounding with the developmental and family context factors, intercorrelations within the seven support predictor sets were calculated. More specifically, both the simple

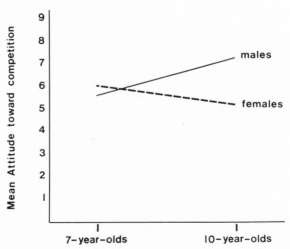

FIG. 2.—Sex × age interaction of attitudes toward competition

correlations between the number of independent variables and the partial (residual) correlations between these variables with controls for the influence of sex, age, sex of sibling, family size, and SES (the control variables) were calculated.

Within sets, individual variables were excluded if their presence yielded a pattern of high collinearity as well as apparent conceptual redundancy. This occurred in three instances, so the variables that indicated the number of peer-, pet-, and parent-generation individuals identified among the 10 most important individuals to the child interviewed were eliminated. Other variables such as intimate talks with grandparents were retained even though their distributions were extremely skewed and/or peaked. These factors would operate in such a fashion as to reduce the probability of attaining statistical significance as predictor variables. The resulting 20 support categories were organized in the following seven sets of possible predictors of social-emotional functioning.

   I. Peer support
      A. Know and interact with peers
      B. Intimate talks with peers
  II. Pet support
      A. Pets as special friends
      B. Intimate talks with pets
 III. Parent-generation support
      A. Know and interact with adult generation
      B. Special talks with adults
      C. Intimate talks with parent generation
  IV. Involvement with parents' jobs as support
      A. Involvement with father's work
      B. Involvement with mother's work
   V. Grandparent-generation support
      A. Know and interact with grandparent generation
      B. Grandparent generation among the 10 most important individuals
      C. Intimate talks with grandparent generation
  VI. Intrapersonal sources of support
      A. Hobbies
      B. Structured fantasies
      C. Unstructured fantasies
      D. Skill development and expression
 VII. Environmental sources of support
      A. Places to get off to by self
      B. Formally sponsored organizations—structured activities
      C. Formally sponsored organizations—unstructured activities
      D. Informal, unsponsored meeting places

TABLE 6

SUMMARY TABLE OF DEVELOPMENTAL, SEX OF CHILD, AND FAMILY-CONTEXT
VARIABLES IN INTERACTION WITH SUPPORT FACTORS PREDICTING
SOCIAL-EMOTIONAL FUNCTIONING

A. DEVELOPMENTAL CONSIDERATIONS

Support Factor	Younger	Older	Social-Emotional Functioning
More intimate talks with pets	Less	More	Empathic
More intimate talks with pets	Less (males)	More (males)	Accepting of individual differences
More intimate talks with pets	Less	More	Competitive
More pets as special friends	More	Less	Competitive
More intimate talks with peers	More	Less	Individualistic
More involved in mother's work	Less	More	Accepting of individual differences
More involvement in formally sponsored organizations with unstructured activities	Less	More	Social perspective taking skill

B. FAMILY CONTEXT

Support Factor	Small Families	Large Families	Social-Emotional Functioning
More knowing and interacting with adults	Less	More	Empathic
More intimate talks with grandparent generation	Less	More	Empathic
More grandparent generation in top ten	Less	More	Internal locus of control
More intimate talks with pets	More	Less	Competitive
More places to get off to by self	More	Less	Accepting of individual differences
More informal, unsponsored meeting places	More	Less	Accepting of individual differences
More involvement in formally sponsored organizations (involving both structured and unstructured activities)	More	Less	Individualistic

TABLE 6 (*Continued*)

C. CONSIDERATIONS OF SEX OF CHILD

Support Factor	Male	Female	Social-Emotional Functioning
More knowing and interacting with adults	More	Less	Social perspective taking skill
More knowing and interacting with adults	More	Less	Internal locus of control
More knowing and interacting with grandparent generation	More	Less	Social perspective taking skill
More knowing and interacting with grandparent generation	More	Less	Empathic
More knowing and interacting with grandparent generation	Less (younger) More (older)	More (younger) Less (older)	Internal locus of control
More intimate talks with grandparent generation	More	Less	Social perspective taking skill
More special talks with adults	Less	More	Internal locus of control
More grandparent generation in top ten	Less	More	Empathic
More informal, unsponsored meeting places	More (younger) Less (older)	Less	Competitive

Next, to consider the specific predictive value of children's report of sources of support, each of the six dependent measures of social-emotional functioning (empathy, acceptance of individual differences, attitudes toward competition, attitudes toward individualism, locus of control, and social perspective taking) was regressed on each set of predictor variables in seven (though not necessarily statistically independent) hierarchical regressions. In each of these hierarchical regressions, a set of five developmental and/or familial context control variables was entered first. These control variables included sex of the child, age, family size, and sex of sibling, which were dichotomous variables, and SES, which was a continuous variable. Then, to consider how support factors per se plus developmental and familial context in conjunction with support factors add to the prediction of social-emotional functioning, over and above the simple additive effects of the control variables, the support variables were entered (as a set), followed, in subsequent steps, by the sex × support interaction; the age × support interaction; the family size × support interaction; the sex × age, sex × family size, and age × family size interactions; and, finally, the sex × age × support interaction.

Individual variables within sets (either main effects or interactions) were examined further only if the set had offered a significant increment in the R^2 at its point of entry (Model II error, ANOVA approach, Cohen & Cohen, 1975). The contribution of individual variables was assessed by controlling for all previously entered variables plus the other variables in that set at that step. To identify situations in which collinearity between variables lead to redundancy, partial correlations were examined that controlled for all previously entered variables but not for the other variables in that set at that step. The F tests used to test the significance of these partial correlations will be reported only in situations in which redundancy was operating. Additionally, where significant interactions appeared, Johnson-Neyman (Kerlinger & Pedhazur, 1973) comparisons were made and regression lines were determined in order to aid interpretation. The results of each of the regressions for each dependent variable will now be presented. Following this report of the usefulness of specific forms of support for predicting social-emotional functioning, findings relevant to selected networks of support will be presented. Finally, results of these regressions will be summarized in accord with issues concerning sources of support by themselves and in interaction with developmental and family context in predicting social-emotional functioning. Along with this summary, consider the predictive value of each set of support variables. Table 6 summarizes all the interactions that follow and organizes these findings according to consideration of age, sex, and family size of the child.

PEER SUPPORT

Report of intimate talks with peers interacted with age of the child to predict attitudes toward individualism, $F(1,156) = 8.34, p < .01$. Whereas the greater reporting of intimate peer relations was associated with lower individualism among 10-year-olds, $F(1,87) = 4.95, p < .05$, the opposite was true for 7-year-olds, $F(1,63) = 3.99, p < .05$. The peer-support set of variables did not reliably predict the remaining five dependent variables considered (empathy, acceptance of individual differences, attitudes toward competition, social perspective taking skill, and locus of control).

PET SUPPORT

Intimate talks with pets interacted with age as a reliable predictor of empathy, $F(1,156) = 5.81$, $p < .05$. Figure 3 illustrates this interaction. While there was a positive slope for the 10-year-olds, there was a negative slope for the 7-year-olds. Greater reporting of intimate talks with pets was associated with higher empathy scores for the 10-year-olds, but the opposite was the case for 7-year-olds.

Intimate talks with pets interacted with sex and age to predict acceptance of individual differences reliably, $F(1,149) = 5.77$, $p < .05$. It is important to keep in mind that a low score on this measure indicated much acceptance of individual differences. The slope of the first-grade males was positive, while the slope of the 10-year-old males was negative. Ten-year-old males, then, who reported having more intimate talks with pets were more accepting of individual differences, whereas the opposite was true for 7-year-old males. (While neither of these slopes was significantly nonzero, the difference between the slopes was reliable.) The slopes of the females at both age groups were negligible.

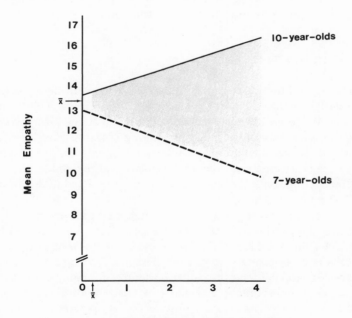

Mean Intimate Talks with Pets

Fig. 3.—Analysis of interaction between age and intimate talks with pets for empathy. Shading indicates 95% confidence interval by Johnson-Neyman criterion.

51

Intimate talks with pets interacted with family size to predict attitudes toward competition reliably, $F(1,154) = 6.23$, $p < .05$. While the slope for large family size was significantly negative, $F(1,73) = 6.59$, $p < .05$, the slope for small family size was positive but negligible. In other words, children from large families were less likely to be competitive in attitude the more they reported intimate talks with pets. This did not hold for children in small families. Reporting the experience of having pets as special friends interacted with age to predict attitudes toward competition reliably as well, $F(1,156) = 4.85$, $p < .05$. Intimate talks with pets also interacted with age to predict attitudes toward competition, $F(1,156) = 3.85$, $p < .05$. The interactions appeared to operate in opposing fashion. While the slope based on intimate talks with pets for the 10-year-olds was positive, it was significantly negative for the 7-year-olds, $F(1,63) = 3.97$, $p < .05$. In contrast, the slope based on pets as special friends for the 10-year-olds was negative, while the slope was positive for the 7-year-olds. In other words, among 10-year-olds, reporting more intimate talks with pets was associated with stronger competitive attitudes, whereas experiencing pets as special friends was associated with weaker competitive attitudes. The opposite was found for 7-year-olds.

Pet support did not reliably predict social perspective taking skill, attitudes toward individualism, or locus of control.

PARENT GENERATION SUPPORT

Knowing and interacting with adults interacted with family size to predict empathy reliably, $F(1,150) = 6.66$, $p < .05$. Figure 4 illustrates this interaction. While the slope for the small families was negative, the slope for the large families was positive. While, among children who knew and interacted with fewer than four neighborhood adults, children from small families were more empathic than children from large families, there was no such difference among children who knew and interacted with four or more adults in the neighborhood.

Knowing and interacting with adults interacted with sex of child reliably to predict social perspective taking, $F(1,156) = 6.71$, $p < .05$, and locus of control, $F(1,156) = 5.11$, $p < .05$. More extensive knowing and interacting with adults was associated with greater perspective taking skill and significantly greater internal locus of control orientation among boys, $F(1,76) = 4.62$, $p < .05$, whereas among girls more extensive knowing and interacting with adults was associated with significantly less perspective taking skill, $F(1,76) = 7.21$, $p < .01$, and less internal locus of control. More particularly, with respect to locus of control orientation, among children who knew and interacted with at least seven neighborhood adults, boys demonstrated greater internal locus of control orientation than did girls. While there was

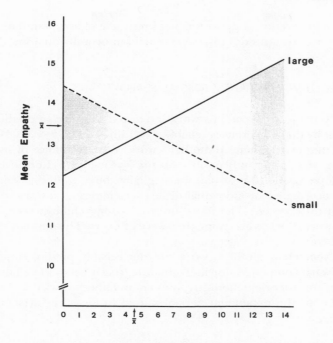

Mean Know and Interact with Adult Generation

Fig. 4.—Analysis of interaction between family size and know and interact with adult generation for empathy. Shading indicates 95% confidence interval by Johnson-Neyman criterion.

no difference in social perspective taking skills among males and females who knew and interacted with four or more adults in their neighborhoods, among children who knew and interacted with fewer than four neighborhood adults, girls demonstrated greater social perspective taking skill than did boys.

Reporting special talks with adults also interacted with the sex of child to predict locus of control orientation, $F(1,156) = 7.05$, $p < .01$. More experience with special talks was associated with a stronger internal locus of control orientation among girls but significantly weaker internal orientation among boys, $F(1,76) = 9.26$, $p < .01$. More specifically, while there was no difference in locus of control orientation among boys and girls who reported two to four adults with whom they have special talks, among children who have no or one adult with whom they have special talks, boys have a stronger internal locus of control than girls, but, among children with five or more adults with whom they have special talks, girls have a stronger internal orientation than do boys.

53

Parent generation support was not predictive of acceptance of individual differences or attitudes toward competition or individualism.

INVOLVEMENT WITH PARENTS' JOBS AS SUPPORT

Involvement with mother's work interacted with age to predict acceptance of individual differences reliably, $F(1,156) = 7.43$, $p < .05$. While the slope relating involvement in mother's work with acceptance of individual differences was significantly positive for the 7-year-olds, $F(1,63) = 6.06$, $p < .05$, the slope for the 10-year-olds was negligible but negative. (Again, a high score for acceptance of individual differences indicated low acceptance of individual differences.) The more involved young children were in their mother's work, the less accepting they were of peers. This was not so for the older children.

Involvement in mother's work did not reliably predict empathy, attitudes toward competition or individualism, social perspective taking skill, or locus of control orientation. Involvement in father's work did not reliably predict any of the dependent variables used to measure social-emotional functioning.

GRANDPARENT GENERATION SUPPORT

Reports of intimate talks with people in the grandparent generation were reliably predictive of empathy, $F(1,159) = 5.16$, $p < .05$. Reports of more intimate talks with persons in the grandparent generation were associated with stronger empathy scores. Reports of having persons in the grandparent generation among the 10 most important individuals in the child's life were found to be redundant with intimate talks with adults in predicting empathy, as illustrated by a significant partial correlation for reports of grandparent generation among the 10 most important individuals, $F(1,161) = 4.09$, $p < .05$. Again, a positive slope was documented.

Intimate talks with grandparents were also found to interact with family size in predicting empathy, $F(1,150) = 5.53$, $p < .05$. Reports of more intimate talks with grandparent generation were associated with higher empathy scores for children in large families, $F(1,72) = 5.00$, $p < .05$, whereas a negligible but inverse relationship among the same variables was found for children in small families. Similarly, reporting the grandparent generation among the 10 most important individuals in the child's life interacted with family size in predicting locus of control orientation, $F(1,153) = 15.59$, $p < .01$. Greater reporting of grandparent generation members among the 10 most important individuals was associated with stronger internal orientation among children in large families but with significantly weaker internal orientation among children in small families, $F(1,70) = 5.23, p < .05$. More specifically, among children who reported no grandparent-generation members in their top ten lists, children in small families had a stronger locus of control than did children in large families. Among children who reported one or two grandparent generation members in their top ten list, there was no difference in locus of control orientation in large versus small families. And finally, among children who reported three or more grandparent generation members in their top ten list, children in large families had a stronger internal locus of control orientation than did children in small families.

Reporting grandparent generation persons among the 10 most important individuals interacted with the sex of the child to predict empathy, $F(1,156) = 8.43, p < .05$. For girls in the sample, experiencing grandparent generation among the 10 most important individuals was significantly and positively related to empathy, $F(1,76) = 10.94, p < .01$. In other words, greater significant involvement with the grandparent generation as reflected by girls' top ten lists was associated with greater empathy. For boys, this relationship was negligible and negative.

Knowing and interacting with the grandparent generation also interacted with the sex of the child to predict empathy, $F(1,156) = 5.68, p < .05$. In this case, the slope for females was significant but negative, $F(1,82) = 4.03, p < .05$, whereas the slope for males was negligible and positive. In other words, greater casual involvement with the grandparent generation was associated with weaker empathy scores for girls but not for boys.

Both knowing and interacting with grandparent generation and intimate talks with persons in the grandparent generation interacted with sex of the child to reliably predict social perspective taking skill, $F(1,156) = 5.21, p < .05$, and $F(1,156) = 9.37, p < .001$, respectively. Both interactions indicate a positive slope for males and a negative slope for females.

Finally, knowing and interacting with the grandparent generation interacted with the sex and age of the child to predict locus of control orientation reliably, $F(1,145) = 4.28, p < .05$. More extensive casual interaction with the grandparent generation was associated with stronger internal orientation for the younger females and the older males but with weaker internal orientation for the older females and the younger males.

Grandparent-generation support did not reliably predict acceptance of individual difference or attitudes toward competition or individualism.

INTRAPERSONAL SOURCES OF SUPPORT

The report of both involvement with hobbies and participation in skill development and expression was associated with greater social perspective taking skill, $F(1,158) = 4.08, p < .05$, and $F(1,158) = 6.97, p < .01$, respectively. Intrapersonal sources of support were not found predictive of empathy, acceptance of individual differences, or attitudes toward competition or individualism.

ENVIRONMENTAL SOURCES OF SUPPORT

Reports of places to get off to by oneself interacted with family size to predict acceptance of individual differences reliably, $F(1,146) = 6.21, p < .05$. While the slope relating reports of places to get off to by oneself to acceptance of individual differences was significant and negative for children in small families, $F(1,67) = 5.29, p < .05$, the comparable slope for children in large families was negligible but positive. For children in small families, this meant that children with several places to get off to by themselves were also more likely to accept individual differences in others than were children without such places. The Johnson-Neyman comparison revealed more specific information. While, among children with just one place to get off to by themselves, children in large families were more accepting of individual differences in others than were children from small families, the reverse was found among children with three or more places to get off to by themselves. That is, when three or more places of independence occurred, children in the small families were more accepting of individual differences than were children in large families.

Reports of informal, unsponsored meeting places also interacted with family size to predict acceptance of individual differences, $F(1,146) = 5.08, p < .05$, as well as attitudes toward individualism, $F(1,146) = 3.89, p < .05$. Among children from small families, reports of more informal, unsponsored meeting places were associated with greater acceptance of peers and decreased individualism, whereas the opposite was true for children from large families. The Johnson-Neyman comparison also revealed that, among children who reported at least six informal, unsponsored meeting places, children from small families were more accepting of individual differences than were children from large families.

Reports of informal, unsponsored meeting places also interacted with sex and age to predict attitudes toward competition, $F(1,139) = 9.51, p < .01$. While reports of more informal, unsponsored meeting places were associated with more competitive attitudes for 7-year-old males, $F(1,24) = 9.60, p < .05$, the opposite was found for 10-year-old males and both age groups of females. More specifically, among the 7-year-olds who reported less than two informal, unsponsored meeting places, girls were more competitive than boys; there was no such difference in competitive attitude among the 7-year-olds who participated in two or more informal, unsponsored meeting places. Among all the boys in the study who reported five or fewer informal, unsponsored meeting places, the 10-year-old boys were more competitive than the 7-year-old boys. Boys in both age groups who participated in more than five informal, unsponsored meeting places did not differ in competitiveness. Regardless of level of involvement in informal, unsponsored meeting places among the 10-year-olds, boys expressed greater competitiveness than did girls.

With respect to formally sponsored organizations, involvement in those offering either structured or unstructured activities interacted with the child's family size to predict attitudes toward individualism, $F(1,146) = 4.28$, $p < .05$, and $F(1,146) = 6.41$, $p < .05$, respectively. In both instances, more extensive involvement with formally sponsored organizations was associated with increased individualism for children in small families (significantly so for greater participation in organizations with unstructured activities, $F[1,167] = 6.40$, $p < .05$), whereas the opposite was found for children in large families. Reports of participation in formally sponsored organizations with unstructured activities interacted with the age of the child to predict social perspective taking skill reliably, $F(1,150) = 8.82$, $p < .01$. Greater participation in formally sponsored organizations with unstructured activities was associated with greater social perspective taking skill among the 10-year-olds, $F(1,83) = 7.07$, $p < .01$, but with negligible and less perspective taking skill among the 7-year-olds. Figure 5 illustrates this interaction.

Environmental sources of support were not predictive of empathy or locus of control.

NETWORK OF SUPPORT

A summary analysis considered the network of potentially important predictors derived from the seven different aspects of support just considered. Since the above analyses are not necessarily independent, the variables that reached significance in the earlier analyses were combined into a single hierarchical regression—a reduced or "estimation" model—that cut across the sets of support. Given that the partial correlations for these variables had only varied between .13 and .31, there was concern that, if these support variables among the seven support sets were redundant with one another, the overall predictive value of support variables would indeed only account for a small (even if statistically significant) portion of the variance in scores found among the six dependent variables. On the other hand, it was hypothesized earlier that a network of support would be more predictive of social-emotional functioning than any one support category.

Thus a reduced model was considered for each of the dependent variables. Entered in the first step were the previously entered control variables

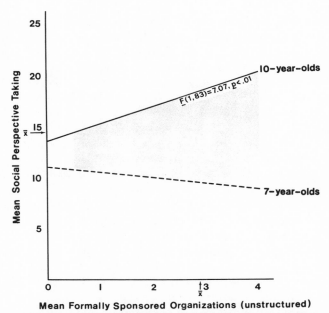

Fɪɢ. 5.—Analysis of interaction between age and formally sponsored organizations (unstructured) for social perspective taking. Shading indicates 95% confidence interval by Johnson-Neyman criterion.

of sex of child, age, family size, sex of sibling, and SES as well as the relevant control variables associated with these selected variables that had attained significance in the individual sets of regressions. Entered in the second step were the specific, select variables that attained significance in the individual, hierarchical regressions. While the networks of support relevant to each of the six dependent variables differed from one another, the selected network of support variables relevant to each dependent variable (e.g., social perspective taking, empathy, etc.) added significantly to the predictability of each of the measures of social-emotional functioning above and beyond what the control variables were able to predict. Appendix H presents the results of these regressions testing the value of a network of sources of support and organizes a summary of particular support variables relevant to each measure of social-emotional functioning.

SUMMARY AND IMPLICATIONS OF FINDINGS

The findings basically confirm the value of pursuing an understanding about children's reported sources of support in their lives. Selected networks of support are predictive of the social-emotional functioning among children living with presumably low- or ordinary-stress conditions in relatively secure American environments. While knowledge of particular sources of support does not individually account for much variance in predicting aspects of social-emotional functioning, knowledge of a selected network of support in conjunction with control variables resulted in R's ranging from .39 for predicting attitudes toward individualism to .78 for predicting social perspective taking. Thus it appears that developing a bridge to community resources and having social supports are related to expressions of enhanced social-emotional functioning. Such a formulation is congruent with the work of Caplan and Grunebaum (1967), Hamburg and Adams (1967), Rapoport (1962), and Viney (1976) and supports Murphy and Moriarty's (1976) notion that children in stable family and neighborhood settings benefit from freedom and opportunities to explore varied experiences. One such developmental opportunity that, to date, has rarely received recognition is intimate involvement with pets during childhood (MacDonald, 1979). The findings in the present study are congruent with the position of Levinson (1978) that animal companions can act as an environmental feature that can make a unique contribution to a child's social/personality development (e.g., the expression of empathy), particularly during middle childhood.

That several of the selected network support variables involved skewed distributions with high kurtosis (e.g., intimate talks with grandparents were absent for most children) documents an empirical basis for concern as to the nature and extent of existing sources of support available to the children in this study. This was true for access and involvement with the grandparent generation in particular. Involvement with potential extended family resources, even in the relatively stable group of families studied, was particularly limited. Even though access to and involvement with grandparents were limited for the sample in this study, involvement with these extended family members was predictive of certain developmental considerations. These findings highlight the value of Hagestad and Speicher's (1981) call for considering the role of grandparents in the development of not only young (infant and preschool) grandchildren but also older grandchildren.

Overall, these findings pertaining to selected networks of support and their power in predicting social-emotional functioning support two earlier formulations. First, networks of support are relevant for children developing in normal, healthy environments (i.e., in relatively low stress settings), not just in highly stressful settings. This study provides baseline data for further research aimed at understanding development under highly stressful conditions. Second, that support variables individually account for little variance in scores of social-emotional functioning and yet in combination with other support variables account for a moderate amount of the variance in the scores of social-emotional functioning cautions us against quick, unidimensional intervention strategies that focus on a single support factor. Findings pertaining to networks of support bolster this report's earlier formulation that existing important sources of support that extend beyond biological endowments and early mother-child relationships are especially relevant to children in middle childhood.

In addition to direct age and sex effects in predicting some of the targeted measures of social-emotional functioning, several other substantive themes emerge from the results of this study. Three such themes focus on age, family size, and sex of the child, and each appears to hold its own developmental significance.

DEVELOPMENTAL CONSIDERATIONS

First, the relationship of support variables to measures of social-emotional functioning frequently operated in a different fashion for the 7-year-olds than it did for the 10-year-olds. When age interacted with support variables, the interaction typically reflected what can be construed as effective use of the support variable, leading to enhanced social-emotional functioning among the 10-year-olds but not among the 7-year-olds. For example, increased levels of participation in formally sponsored organizations with unstructured activities was related to increased levels of social perspective taking for the 10-year-olds but not for the 7-year-olds. A second example in this study indicates that the relationship between reporting intimate talks with pets and empathy was positive for the 10-year-olds but negative for the 7-year-olds. Thus greater intimate involvement with pets was reflected in higher empathy scores for the older children and lower empathy scores for the younger children in the study. A third example involves the child's reported involvement with his or her mother's work and acceptance of individual differences. Greater involvement with mother's work was associated with lesser acceptance of individual differences among the 7-year-olds, but this seemingly adverse relationship did not hold among the 10-year-olds. There are other examples, but what is noteworthy is that age of the child interacted with a support dimension in a comparable fashion for each of the six dependent measures regressed on the support dimensions, and these interactions, with cautious interpretation of cultural norms regarding attitudes toward competition and individualism, suggested an experience of adversity among the 7-year-olds and neutrality or enhanced social-emotional functioning among the 10-year-olds.

R. Lazarus (personal communication, 1979) differentiates social support from coping in that one may have social support resources but not employ them to ameliorate stress. What we may be seeing in these data is the outcome of successful coping and utilization of support resources among the 10-year-olds. This is implying cause and effect with basically correlational data, but the data do suggest a provocative developmental process worth further investigation. A second interpretation of these interactions with age is that, over time, the experiences of the support dimensions take effect, and so we see positive "outcomes" in the 10-year-old data. Longitudinal follow-up of the 7-year-olds would provide a test for such a "sleeper" effect. A third interpretation was suggested in the introductory section of this report. Pause to consider that continued development into adolescence may find sleeper effects in the data obtained from 10-year-olds as well but that, without data from a contrast group, such potential effects are not apparent. This third perspective argues for the relevance of challenge and push from the "parental nest" for 10-year-olds that may not be so relevant for the younger children. Parental support may be more critical in the early years, while parental distance in later middle childhood may facilitate one's productive involvement with other sources of support. Regardless of which interpretation(s) one follows, these findings highlight developmental activity during middle childhood.

FAMILY CONTEXT

Family size was a structural, contextual element of the family experience that appears to moderate the experience of certain sources of support as they operate to predict social-emotional functioning. Such a phenomenon held for five of the six dependent measures considered, including empathy, acceptance of individual differences, attitudes toward competition and individualism, and locus of control orientation. For example, knowing and interacting with adults and intimate involvement with the grandparent generation showed a positive relationship with empathy among children in large families but a negative relationship with empathy among children in small families. Supplemental involvement with the adult generations, both parent and grandparent, appears useful to children in large families but not useful to children in small families.

What is more critically useful to children in small families appears to be opportunities for independence from the nuclear family. For the children in small families in this study, reporting opportunity to get off by themselves away from their families, be it alone or with others in informal settings away from home, was related to increased acceptance of individual differences in others. This relationship did not hold for the children in large families. Thus it appears that experiencing privacy, autonomy, and independence from one's nuclear family, especially the adult generation of that nuclear family, reflects enhanced social-emotional functioning among children in small families.

This observed differential role that is associated with experiencing supplemental involvement with the adult generation and experiencing autonomy from the nuclear family may well be rooted in a differential intensity of affective involvement with and supervision by mothers and fathers experienced by children in small as compared to large families. Highly intense and early exclusive involvement with one's mother, in particular, may be more characteristic of children's experience in small families as compared to large families. The cross-cultural data obtained by Mead (1928) and Ainsworth (1967) suggest that intensity of affect with mothers is inversely related to the number of available caretakers (regardless of age of caretaker). This also fits Bossard and Boll's (1956) formulation that parents in large families, by distributing their time and energy among the various family members, are not as likely to require or engage as strong an emotional interaction with any one child as is true of parents with a small number of children. Indeed, Belle and Longfellow (1983) report that children were more likely to report themselves lonely when they lived in a household context with a high ratio of children to adults. Thus it appears that, where parental involvement is intense, opportunities for breaking away from this intense involvement, at least at times, is related to enhanced social-emotional functioning. Similarly, for children in families where parental involvement is not so intense, developing supplemental relationships with other adults is related to enhanced social-emotional functioning. Such a formulation warrants a clearer test of this phenomenon than is offered by the present study. As noted by Werner (1979), we know relatively little about the specific effects of auxiliary caretakers, varying in age and status, on the social development of children. The findings of this study argue for the value of studying this issue even in our culture, in which we have a relatively narrow view of who are our children's caretakers.

SEX OF CHILD CONSIDERATIONS

Sex of the child is a third variable that moderated the relationship between the experience of sources of support and psychological well-being, and this appeared to occur for all but one measure of social-emotional functioning. The one exception involved attitudes toward individualism. Extensiveness of casual involvement with persons in the adult generations, both parent and grandparent generations, resulted in special significance for the boys in this study. Extensive, casual involvement, not intensive, intimate involvement, with adults was positively linked to social perspective taking skill and internal locus of control orientation among boys but negatively related to this skill and orientation among girls. Extensive and intensive involvement with the grandparent generation was positively related to the social perspective taking skill in boys and negatively related to this skill in girls. Extensive, casual involvement with the grandparent generation was related to greater expression of empathy among boys and lower empathy among girls. Intensive involvement with the grandparent generation, on the other hand, was positively linked to increased expression of empathy among the girls but not among the boys in this study. Intensive relationships with adults were also positively linked with an internal locus of control orientation among the girls but not among the boys. In sum, not only do boys and girls appear to differ in the extent to which they seek out, respond to, and report extensive (i.e., casual) versus intensive (i.e., intimate) relationships with others, as reported earlier in this report and as previously found by both Berndt (1981) and Waldrop and Halverson (1975), these experiences of extensive/casual and intensive/intimate relationships appear to have different developmental correlates for the two sexes.

IMPLICATIONS FOR UNDERSTANDING THE DEVELOPMENT OF SPECIFIC ASPECTS OF SOCIAL-EMOTIONAL FUNCTIONING

As noted earlier, the Neighborhood Walk support variables (e.g., intimate talks with grandparent generation) individually account for little variance in scores of social-emotional functioning, making it unwise to focus on single support factors to predict any given aspect of social-emotional functioning. Additionally, individual child factors (i.e., age and sex of child) as well as family context (i.e., family size) rather systematically moderate how support variables operate to predict aspects of social-emotional functioning. With these qualifications in mind, we can concentrate attention on those cases in which a pattern is suggested by the analyses of support factors in regard to predicting particular aspects of social-emotional functioning.

For example, factors involving grandparents were particularly salient in predicting empathy (e.g., know and interact with grandparent generation × sex of child, grandparent generation among 10 most important individuals × sex of child, intimate talks with grandparent generation, intimate talks with grandparent generation × family size). Involvement with pets and the parent generation was also relevent in predicting empathy. What the grandparent generation and pet "generation" have in common for empathy development may be unconditional, special acceptance of children and their feelings or relationships with unfrightening opportunities for exploring and acknowledging feelings of selves and others.

With respect to children's view of locus of control, the adult generation, both parent and grandparent, appears particularly salient. Both casual and intimate experiences with the adult generation were related to a child's perceived locus of control orientation.

In contrast, opportunities for independence from adults to be with peers or to be in privacy or engaged with pets were particularly relevant for children's acceptance of individual differences among their peers.

Attitudes toward both competition and individualism appear related to children's experiences with peers (inside and/or outside of organizations). It may be that, under certain circumstances, relationships with pets can have aspects of "peer" relationships as involvement with pets was also predictive of one's attitudes toward competition.

Finally, the configuration of support factors associated with social perspective taking is unique in comparison to the other measures analyzed in this study by the association found between this aspect of social-emotional functioning and intrapersonal sources of support, that is, experience with skill development and expression as well as experience with hobbies. In addition to these unique factors, involvement with peers in formally sponsored organizations with unstructured activities appears to be associated with greater social perspective taking for some children. What is common to all these factors is at least indirect parental support—that is, money for supplies involved with hobbies and lessons often involved with skill development as well as tax/bond support for formally sponsored organizations. Parents have also been known to guide children into hobbies and skill development activities. These factors may also involve special cognitive challenges relevant to social perspective taking skill. How these indirect parental factors as well as the activities themselves yield an association to social perspective taking warrants further consideration.

DESIGN CONSIDERATIONS OF ADULT-SPONSORED SUPPORT

Finally, the resulting selected networks of support relevant for predicting social-emotional functioning have an interesting implication for the value or design of formally sponsored organizations intended to promote the development of psychological well-being. Involvement in formally sponsored organizations with structured activities was not found predictive of any of the measures of social-emotional functioning considered in this study. Participation in informal, unsponsored meeting places under certain conditions was predictive of acceptance of individual differences and attitudes toward competition. Unstructured opportunities to get away by oneself were, under certain conditions also, predictive of acceptance of individual differences. Participation in hobbies and skill development and expression were also positively related to social perspective taking skill. And, finally, participation in formally sponsored organizations with unstructured activities was predictive of the social perspective taking skill of certain children. Overall, then, it appears that environmental settings and organizations that allow the child to experience autonomy, control, and mastery of the content of the activity are related to expressions of enhanced social-emotional functioning on the part of the child. This formulation is congruent with Werner and Smith's (1982) finding that children and their families preferred to seek help from an informal network of kin, neighbors, teachers, and ministers rather than from the more formally structured professional, mental health establishments. The data from the present study lead me to conclude (at least tentatively so), as Werner and Smith conclude from data obtained from children from a wider range of SES and representing more predominantly different ethnic groups than was characteristic of the sample in the present study, that it appears to make better sense to strengthen or foster informal ties to kin and community rather than to focus resources on establishing and developing formal organizations and structured activities per se for the delivery of social services to children in middle childhood. Recognition of the value of the child's experience of autonomy (especially overt autonomy from adults) as well as relatedness to others is also called for by these data.

A clue as to how to approach enhancing informal sources of support for children in middle childhood comes from a 7-year-old interviewed for this report. This 7-year-old freely "interrupted" the interview by taking note and sharing with the adult interviewer the whereabouts and activities of his cat's friend, another cat that remained otherwise unnamed. To avoid telling a shaggy dog story about a cat, his cat's friend ended up as the third most important individual and special friend in this child's life. When asked what made his cat's friend special, this serious young 7-year-old slowly revealed, "Well, it's kind of hard to explain, but my cat's friend kind of respects me." So who might a 7-year-old turn to for respect? The findings of the present study suggest that adults are well advised to listen to "our" children for the answer. In other words, enhancing informal sources of support for children in middle childhood requires adults to listen to the young very carefully and have considerable regard for their perspective.

VII. CONSIDERATION OF ACCESSIBILITY OF SOURCES OF SUPPORT

In the previous chapter, the actual accessibility of sources of support was not directly addressed. No distinction was made between children being able to walk or bike to a resource and their needing someone to take them there by car, bus, or other forms of public transportation. In this chapter, accessibility of sources of support is considered.

First, to provide a descriptive understanding of the accessibility of specific sources of support, Table 7 presents the percentage of sources of support to which children could walk, bike, take a car, bus, train, plane, or other. It is clear that most sources of support tapped by the Neighborhood Walk are indeed in the neighborhood and easily accessible (walk or bike) to children. Still, for certain experiences many children in the study had to rely on others for access. Among others, this held for access to grandparents, belonging to formal organizations, playing with cousins, and getting to father's place of work.

Next, scores regarding involvement in special talks with adults, hobbies, skill development and expression, places to get off to by oneself, and formally sponsored organizations with both structured and unstructured activities were revised to include only those involvements that were accessible by walking or biking. In other words, sources of support were considered clearly accessible if the child could walk or bike to these individuals and places. These revised scores were substituted in the seven sets of support categories and reanalyzed following the same procedures described in Chapter VI. One additional score was derived and used as a covariate in the grandparent-generation support set of variables. This score simply measured the extent to which each set of grandparents and any other grandparent generation individuals that the children reported visiting were indeed accessible. Test-retest reliability for these accessibility-based sources of support were again high (r ranged between .83 and .97), and percent of exact agreement or of being off by 1 point ranged between 95% and 100%.

Three-way analyses of variance for unequal N's were completed, with

TABLE 7

Accessibility: Percent of Cases for Most Accessible Way to Support

Specific Questions on Neighborhood Walk[a]	Walk	Bike	Car	Bus	Train	Plane	Other	N[b]
1. Special place to be alone	93	7	…	…	…	…	…	148
2. Best friend	29	43	25	…	…	3	…	162
3. Play with kids away from school	38	54	8	…	…	…	…	144
4. Special friend	39	34	23	1	…	2	1	112
5. Visit adults in neighborhood	75	20	5	…	…	…	…	133
6. Visit adults who no longer work	36	15	48	…	…	1	…	75
7. Visit grandparents	5	3	78	…	0[c]	14	…	245
8. Teacher talk outside class	62	20	15	4	…	…	…	109
9. Belong to informal organizations	70	26	4	…	…	…	…	54
10. Belong to formal organizations	5	33	60	2	…	…	…	129
11. Go to church, library, etc.	36	28	36	1	…	…	…	1,007
12. Go to store for present	5	26	66	2	…	…	…	149
13. Talk to neighbors	97	3	…	…	…	…	…	162
14. Go visiting with mother and father	21	1	78	…	…	…	…	148
15. Play with cousins	7	5	79	10	…	…	…	155
16. Father's job	2	7	90	1	…	…	…	163
17. Mother's job	44	13	40	3	…	…	…	152
18. What like about school	34	39	15	13	…	…	…	168
19. Lessons out/in school	22	28	47	3	…	…	…	102
20. Hobbies	44	17	39	…	…	…	…	188
21. Go to movies	5	8	87	…	…	…	…	133
22. Arts and crafts	67	17	12	5	…	…	…	237
23a. Watch TV	100	…	…	…	…	…	…	167
23b. Listen to radio	100	…	…	…	…	…	…	121

NOTE.—Percentages are based on the number of times a response occurred.

[a] See App. B for exact wording of questions.

[b] N = number of times a response occurred (a child could give more than one response).

[c] One response.

SES included as a covariate for the seven accessibility scores. There was a significant sex of child effect for accessibility to hobbies, $F(1,159) = 5.67$, $p < .05$. An age effect was documented for accessibility of skill development and expression, $F(1,159) = 14.22$, $p < .001$, accessibility of places to get off to by oneself, $F(1,159) = 21.55$, $p < .001$, and accessibility to both structured and unstructured activities at formally sponsored organizations, $F(1,159) = 11.62$, $p < .05$, and $F(1,159) = 10.29$, $p < .01$, respectively. Appendix I presents the means and standard deviations of the accessibility scores broken down by age group and also presents the obtained ranges for the scores with respect to the entire sample.

After each of the six dependent variables (empathy, acceptance of individual differences, attitudes toward competition and individualism, social perspective taking, and locus of control orientation) was regressed on each set of accessibility predictor variables, reduced models of predictor variables were selected in the same manner as described in Chapter VI. Previously selected variables from predictor sets not subject to accessibility modification were retained in the reduced models. Table 8 presents the resulting multiple R's for these reduced model analyses. A reduced model for the prediction of attitudes toward competition was not considered because no accessibility variable was predictive of scores on this measure.

Finally, to determine whether accessibility of sources of support made a significant contribution to the predictability of enhanced social-emotional functioning, an expanded, two-step reduced model was completed. The first step included the full reduced model reported in the preceding chapter; the second step included any additional variables (and their controls) that resulted from the accessibility regressions. Accessibility scores, as a set, significantly increased the predictability of acceptance of individual differences, $F(6,146) = 3.15$, $p < .01$, attitudes toward individualism, $F(8,142) = 3.31$, $p < .01$, and social perspective taking, $F(8,144) = 2.14$, $p < .05$, but did not significantly increase the predictability of empathy or locus of control orientation. In these expanded regressions, the multiple R became .50 for locus of control orientation, .55 for both acceptance of individual differences and attitudes toward individualism, .60 for empathy, and .80 for social perspective taking skill.

In addition to consideration of accessibility measures per se, several significant interactions occurred that were not suggested by the earlier regressions. Table 9 identifies these interactions. To illustrate these results, it was found that involvement in both structured and unstructured fantasy was, under certain conditions, predictive of aspects of social-emotional functioning. For example, involvement with structured fantasy interacted with sex of the child to predict acceptance of individual differences reliably. The slope based on involvement in structured fantasy was positive for girls and negative for boys. Involvement with unstructured fantasy interacted with

TABLE 8

MULTIPLE R's AND THEIR ASSOCIATED TESTS OF SIGNIFICANCE FOR REDUCED MODEL REGRESSIONS,
INCLUDING SCORING OF ACCESSIBILITY FOR SELECTED NETWORK OF SUPPORT

Predicted Variable	$R_{control}$	pR_{select}	F for pR_{select}	R_{total}	F for R_{total}
Empathy	.44	.45	$F(7,146) = 5.34, p < .001$	.60	$F(21,146) = 3.82, p < .001$
Acceptance of individual differences	.35	.41	$F(5,149) = 6.13, p < .001$	.52	$F(18,149) = 3.10, p < .001$
Social perspective taking skill	.71	.45	$F(7,150) = 5.40, p < .001$	.78	$F(17,150) = 13.50, p < .001$
Locus of control (z score)	.31	.37	$F(3,156) = 7.92, p < .001$	.44	$F(11,156) = 3.34, p < .001$
Attitudes toward individualism	.32	.39	$F(5,147) = 5.23, p < .001$	.49	$F(20,147) = 2.27, p < .001$

TABLE 9

SUMMARY OF "NEW" INTERACTIONS RESULTING FROM ACCESSIBILITY REGRESSIONS

A. SEX OF CHILD

Support Category	Male	Female	Social-Emotional Functioning
More structured fantasy[a]	Less	More	Acceptance of individual differences
Access to special talks with adults	Less	More	Internal locus of control orientation
Access to hobbies[b]	More (older) Less (younger)	Less (older) More (younger)	Individualistic

B. FAMILY SIZE

Support Category	Small	Large	Social-Emotional Functioning
More unstructured fantasy[c]	More	More	Social perspective taking skill
Access to skill	More	Less	Individualistic
Access to formal organizations— structured	More	Less	Individualistic

[a] Especially true for older children.
[b] Especially true for females.
[c] Especially strong for children in small families.

family size to predict social perspective taking skill reliably. The slope for children from both large and small families was positive, but the slope for children in small families was steeper. That these variables were not so identified in the earlier regressions suggests problems of collinearity that led to suppression.

DISCUSSION

These findings have implications for the usefulness of measuring accessibility of reported sources of support. Comparison of the R's resulting from the reduced models simply using and not using accessibility scores—respectively, $R_{total} = .60$ versus .57 for empathy, $R_{total} = .52$ versus .46 for acceptance of individual differences, $R_{total} = .49$ versus .39 for individualism, $R_{total} = .44$ versus .49 for locus of control orientation, and $R_{total} =$

.78 versus .78 for social perspective taking skill—indicates that the additional time spent to obtain accessibility information does not necessarily effect significantly greater predictablity of social-emotional functioning. When one uses both kinds of scoring procedures in combination, however, then accessibility scores significantly increased the predictability of acceptance of individual differences, individualism, locus of control orientation, and social perspective taking skill. In other words, measures of accessibility carry with them some meaningful information that is not entirely redundant with the support measures that do not consider accessibility. If used in combination with other types of measures of support, then, accessibility measures might be worth the added effort and expense.

In sum, although children have easy access to a wide range of support resources, they are nonetheless, in part, dependent in middle childhood on others to provide accessibility to certain resources, some of which increase the value of sources of support in predicting social-emotional functioning.

VIII. POTENTIAL CONFOUNDING FACTORS

LENGTH OF RESIDENCE IN RELATION TO REPORTED SUPPORT

Although children represented in this study had lived at their current address for an average of 5.92 years (SD = 4.18), these children had had varying amounts of time to garner ongoing sources of support in the neighborhoods. To consider the role that length of residence in the neighborhood played in relation to reported sources of support, simple correlations were calculated on the basis of the number of years a child lived at his or her current address and each support category. Although results pertaining to statistically significant correlations will be discussed, all the relations pertaining to length of residence were weak.

Children's greater lengths of residence at a given address were associated with children knowing and interacting with more adults in the neighborhood, $r(166) = .16, p < .05$, and being more involved in their father's work, $r(166) = .23, p < .01$, but seeking out fewer intimate talks with parent-generation adults, $r(166) = -.13, p < .05$. In other words, children can find peer- and grandparent-generation support more readily than they can casual and work-related parent-generation support. That children require considerable time to get to know the parent generation in their neighborhood and their father's world of work does not tell us whether children are reluctant to introduce themselves to the parent-generation world or whether adults who are working (i.e., parent generation) are reluctant to involve others in their busy, demanding lives. What is clear, however, from these results and those from earlier studies with adults (Fisher et al., 1977) is that both children and adults find that it takes considerable time to become involved "neighbors" with the parent generation.

Children who had lived longer at their current address also reported fewer pets in their top ten lists, $r(166) = -.16, p < .05$. This finding suggests that pets provide special, important support when the child's external environment is relatively fragile and insecure.

More years at the same residence was also associated with more use of structured fantasies, $r(166) = .17$, $p < .05$, and more involvement in formally sponsored organizations with structured activities, $r(166) = .12$, $p < .05$. "Long-term" residents appear to experience more structure in several areas of their lives, relative to children "new" in the neighborhood.

Finally, to check out whether these simple correlations between the support variables and years at current address were actually reflections of other factors related to length of residence, partial correlations between the support variables and years at current address were calculated. These partial correlations controlled for sex of child, age of child, family size, sex of older sibling, and SES. With the exception of formally sponsored organizations with structured activities, where the size of the partial and simple correlations remained the same but the more limited degrees of freedom for the partialing resulted in an insignificant correlation, the findings based on partial correlations were congruent with those derived from simple correlations.

COMMUNITY STATUS IN RELATION TO REPORTED SUPPORT

Not only might length of residence in a particular community be related to the child's network of existing support, but the type of community might also limit or enhance garnering certain types of support. To test this latter consideration, three MANOVAs were completed to consider the possible effects of community (i.e., county seat, university town, rural setting), sex of child, age of child, family size, and sex of sibling in addition to all possible two-way and three-way interactions of these factors in relation to children's reporting of others as sources of support, intrapersonal sources of support, and environmental sources of support. Since the main effects of the control variables (developmental and family-context factors) and their interactions have already been discussed, only those effects involving community status are now reported. The first MANOVA, entering the 15 interpersonal support categories as the dependent variables, yielded neither a significant main community effect nor community interaction effects. The second MANOVA, entering the four intrapersonal support categories as the dependent variables, yielded a community main effect, $F(8,232) = 2.50$, $p < .01$, and an age of child by community interaction effect, $F(8,232) = 2.27$, $p < .05$. The third MANOVA, entering the four environmental support measures as the dependent variables, yielded no main effect for community or any community interaction effects.

Univariate procedures were used to determine which particular intrapersonal support variables were responsible for the significant effects found in these MANOVAs. Post hoc contrasts were considered using Newman-Keuls procedures at a p level of less than .05.

Community status was related to skill development and expression, $F(2,119) = 7.84$, $p < .01$. Children in Community U reported more ($M = 6.86$, SD $= 2.98$) experiences of skill development and expression (e.g., receiving honors, taking lessons) than did children living in either Community CS ($M = 5.29$, SD $= 2.11$) or Community R ($M = 5.40$, SD $= 2.39$). The community main effect was a function of SES as a univariate analysis of this community effect; using SES as a covariate eliminated this community effect. Community status, thus, was confounded with SES in relation to the kind of intrapersonal sources children experience.

Age of the child interacted with community status in relation to children's report of skill development and expression, $F(2,127) = 6.51$, $p < .01$. This interaction effect held even when SES was entered as a covariate, $F(2,126) = 6.42$, $p < .01$. Ten-year-olds in Community U reported more ($M = 8.38$, SD $= 2.79$) involvement with skill development and expression than both the younger children in all three communities (Community CS, $M = 4.72$, SD $= 1.65$; Community U, $M = 4.90$, SD $= 1.90$; Community R, $M = 4.50$, SD $= 1.77$) and the older children in the other two communities (Community CS, $M = 5.75$, SD $= 2.34$; Community R, $M = 6.00$, SD $= 2.63$).

Community status was related to intrapersonal sources of support, although community status in one instance was confounded with socioeconomic factors. Independent of SES, however, the 10-year-olds in Community U were more involved in skill development activities than were those in the rest of the sample. Neither environmental nor interpersonal sources of support were related to the child's community status. The lack of pervasive community effects could, in part, be due to the similarities in the three communities. That there was a trend for a sex of child × community interaction with respect to environmental sources of support, $F(8,232) = 1.85$, $p < .07$, suggests that sampling more disparate communities would have elicited more community differences with respect to children's report of environmental sources of support. There is no immediate indication that this would hold true for interpersonal sources of support. Despite varying population-density factors in the three communities, children were able to garner pet-, peer-, parent-, and grandparent-generation support to comparable degrees in the rural and the town communities studied. Overall, these findings highlight that those sources of support that require adult sanction of skill development and achievement (e.g., music lessons) are more susceptible to community and socioeconomic influences than the more informal sources of support are. It is not surprising that children whose parents choose a university community as a home base are especially involved in skill development and its expression. Also since the adult folklore in the county acclaims the university town as particularly "child oriented," these results from the child's perspective suggest that what adults are identifying as a child-oriented community has to do with activities fostering achievement, not those aspects of the community that foster interpersonal support.

In sum, the extent of a child's network of support is weakly tempered in some respects by the length of the child's residence at a particular address (especially with respect to involvement with the parent generation) and in a limited way by the type of community (e.g., with respect to support sources requiring adult sanction) represented in this study of nonmetropolitan and rural communities. When studying a wide range of communities, these factors might play a larger role in restricting or enhancing the child's experience of support during middle childhood.

IX. SUMMARY

There is a lack of documented information about the sources of support in children's lives and their relation to child development, and there is also cause for concern as to the nature and extent of existing resources. This study documented how children in two middle childhood age groups vary in their perceived access to and interaction with friends, relatives, and "recreational" facilities in their communities by means of a Neighborhood Walk.

One hundred and sixty-eight children participated in this project. Their families were residing in nonmetropolitan and rural northern California at the time of their participation. Of the 168 families who participated in this study, 96 had a target child just finishing the fourth grade, and 72 had a target child just finishing the first grade. Within each age group, there were equal numbers of large families (three or more children) and small families (two children), equal numbers of male and female target children, and equal numbers of older brothers and sisters.

The walk around the neighborhood was intended to elicit cues and reminders so as to encourage accurate and inclusive reporting from children and to create an interview that did not seem like a test. This method relied on the report of children about their experiences and offers a unique child-focused perspective.

Following the Neighborhood Walk, an array of affective and social development measures considered to be aspects of psychological well-being were administered. Factor analyses at the two age levels did not produce comparable underlying factor structures. Seven-year-old children who are at the beginning phase of middle childhood apparently do not experience social and affective phenomena with the same coherence as do children in the latter phase of middle childhood (10-year-olds).

Six measures of social-emotional functioning were considered in subsequent analyses: empathy, acceptance of individual differences, attitudes toward competition, attitudes toward individualism, locus of control orientation, and social perspective taking skill. These measures each represent one of four factors derived for the 7-year-olds and/or the 10-year-olds.

Support was conceptualized to include both experiences of relatedness to others and experiences of autonomy from others. Three major categories of reported support in this study using the Neighborhood Walk were considered: others as resources (e.g., persons in the peer, parent, and grandparent generation; pets), intrapersonal sources of support (e.g., hobbies; fantasies—structured and unstructured; skill development), and environmental sources of support (e.g., places to get off to by oneself; formally sponsored organizations with both structured and unstructured activities; informal, unsponsored meeting places). The Neighborhood Walk procedure of interviewing and scoring provides a reasonably reliable (often quite reliable) means of allowing children in middle childhood to speak for themselves. The extent to which these types of support were reported by children in this study was related to the age, sex, and family size of the children. More specifically, females, as compared to males, experience more intensive relationships and a less extensive, casual network of relationships and make more use of intrapersonal support strategies. Females, then, appear more involved with intimate, intrapsychic phenomena than are males in middle childhood. Furthermore, the social context in which children in small families develop contrasts with that experienced by children in large families: children in small families appear more intimately involved with the parent generation, whereas children in large families appear to garner others among their peer and grandparent generation as well as the pet population, perhaps to compensate for the less intimate involvement with parents or simply further enrich their lives. With respect to the relationship between age and sources of support, middle childhood can be characterized as a period during which children develop more elaborated interpersonal, intrapersonal, and environmental sources of support. Illustrations of the variety of individual child responses remind us that an interview method that allows children to provide content specific to their own lives can still be categorized and interpreted in meaningful ways. Finally, results confirm that the Neighborhood Walk procedure assesses the child's personal experience of sources of support and, as such, is not a collective, sociological measure of neighborhoods but rather an individual, psychological "landscape" of sources of support.

After an initial series of hierarchical regressions led to the selection of support variables predictive of the six criterion measures of social-emotional functioning, a reduced model involving a single hierarchical regression was used to assess the predictive value of the child's selected networks of support variables. The child's perception of available sources of support is relevant to the social-emotional functioning of children growing up in relatively secure and low-stress conditions in modern American society. While knowledge of particular sources of support does not individually account for much variance in predicting aspects of psychological well-being, knowledge

77

of a selected network of support in conjunction with age of child, sex of child, family size, sex of older sibling, SES and, when relevant, accessibility of support resulted in R's ranging from .49 for predicting attitudes toward competition and locus of control orientation to .78 for predicting social perspective taking skill. Thus it does appear that developing a bridge to community resources and having social supports, especially informal support sources, are related to social-emotional functioning during middle childhood. How these "bridges" operate appears to be moderated by the age of the child, sex of the child, and the size of the child's family. More specifically, the relevance of support in predicting social-emotional functioning is greater at age 10 than it is at age 7; while supplemental involvement with the adult generation is predictive of the social-emotional functioning of children from large families, predictive factors for children from small families had to do with opportunities for independence from the nuclear family (especially the adult generation); and not only do boys and girls appear to differ in the extent to which they seek out, respond to, and report extensive (i.e., casual) versus intensive relationships with others, but these experiences of extensive and intensive relationships also appear to have different developmental correlates for the two sexes.

Although children in this study appear to have easy access to a wide range of support resources, they are nonetheless, in part, dependent on others to provide accessibility to certain resources, some of which enhance the value of sources of support in predicting social-emotional functioning. It appears that environmental settings and organizations that allow the child to experience autonomy, control, and mastery of the content of the activity are predictive of expressions of enhanced social-emotional functioning during middle childhood. Recognition of the value of the child's experience of autonomy (especially overt autonomy from adults) as well as relatedness to others is also called for by the data from this study. Further regard for the child's perspective of support is urged.

Finally, results from the child's perspective utilized in the Neighborhood Walk suggest that what adults at times informally identify as child-oriented communities has to do with activities fostering achievement, not those aspects of the community that foster interpersonal support. Children as young as 7 years of age can be reliably interviewed, and their responses are useful in predicting social-emotional functioning.

APPENDIX A

TABLE A1

SAMPLE CHARACTERISTICS DISTINGUISHING COMMUNITIES

SAMPLE CHARACTERISTICS	COMMUNITY CS		COMMUNITY U		COMMUNITY R		F^a	p
	M	SD	M	SD	M	SD		
Total population density	1,359.82	769.19	1,728.07	1,562.86	122.63	152.72	4.16	.05
Child population density	222.60	134.43	131.33	120.87	15.23	18.79	5.89	.01
SES	2.93	.79	1.70	.71	2.75	.91	48.51	.01
Rooms in home (N)	7.30	1.53	8.09	1.63	7.65	1.79	4.28	.05
Years in present county	17.33	11.89	10.14	6.11	15.80	11.34	10.20	.01
Cars owned (N)	2.16	.65	1.94	.75	2.40	1.00	3.49	.05

[a] Degrees of freedom for the comparisons of density were 2 and 15, while degrees of freedom for the other comparisons were 2 and 161.

THE NEIGHBORHOOD WALK

I'd like to find out about kids your age. I want to know what fourth (first)/fifth (second) graders like you like to do around home. To start out, I'd like you to show me around your home and neighborhood.

GENERAL FORMAT QUESTIONS WHEN NEEDED

1. To [do that], do you walk, ride a bike, or go by car or bus?
   (W = walk; B = bike; C = car; O = other [e.g., bus or plane].)
2. Can you go by yourself, or do you need to be with someone when _____?
   (Mark "/" [slash] through W, B, C, or O to indicate that child needs to be with someone, and note with whom.)
3. How often?
   (Every day; once a week; once or twice a month; one to four times a year; once every couple of years or more.)
4. Is that person a relative or a nonrelative?
   (Circle r to indicate a relative, and note nature of relationship.)[5]

[5] The nature of the relationship consists of four factors categorized in the following manner: younger, same age, or older; male or female; immediate relation, extended relation, or nonrelated; and peer generation, parent generation, or grandparent generation. Future formats for the Neighborhood Walk should incorporate these coding categories for easy use by the interviewer.

Today's date _____   Older sib _____
Identification # _____   Small or large family?
Order _____   _____

Tell me. Who is in your family? Who do you live with here at home? _____

Name	Relation	Young/Old
_____	_____	_____
_____	_____	_____
_____	_____	_____
_____	_____	_____
_____	_____	_____

DURING THE WALK

W B C O   1. a. Say you didn't feel like talking with anybody. Do you have a special place to be alone? _____
              b. Where do you go to get off by yourself and think things through?

              _____

W B C O   2. a. Some kids your age don't have any friends. Would you say you have any friends? _____
              b. Do you have a "best friend?"

              _____

              c. How do you get to your "best friend?"

              _____

W B C O   3. a. Do you play with kids away from school? _____
              b. Do you go over to (other) kids' homes to play? _____

        c. How many friends' homes can you go and knock on their door?

        ——————

        d. How many friends' homes can you go inside and play? ——————

W   B   C   O   4. a. Do you have a special friend who is like a brother or sister to you?

        ——————

        b. Is this friend like an older or younger brother/sister? —————— (which if either)

        c. Is this friend a relative like a cousin? ——————

W   B   C   O   5. a. Do you visit grownups (adults) in your neighborhood? ——————
        i. Who? ——————
        ii. Are they relatives of yours?

        ——————

        b. Which adults in your neighborhood do you know? ——————

W   B   C   O   6. a. Do you visit adults who are older and are no longer working?

        ——————

        b. Who are they? ——————
        c. Are they relatives to you?
        —————— Aunts? ——————
        Uncles? —————— Other?

        ——————

W   B   C   O   7. a. Do you visit a grandmother or a grandfather? ——————
        b. Do they live with you? ——————
        c. How often do you visit them?

        ——————

W   B   C   O   8. a. Do you know a teacher whom you like to talk to outside of class?

        ——————

        b. Do you go to the teacher's home?

        ——————

        c. Is this teacher a relative? ——————

W   B   C   O   9. a. Do you belong to any clubs (e.g., forts) in the neighborhood? ——————
        b. What are they? ——————

W   B   C   O   10. a. Do you belong to organizations or teams like Little League, Brownies, Boy Scouts or Girl Scouts, etc.? _____

                              b. What are they? _____

r   W   B   C   O   11. a. Do you go to church or temple? _____ Do you go to parties or groups after Sunday school or church services? _____ Are there adults there you have special talks with? _____ Who? _____

r   W   B   C   O   b. Do you go to the library? _____ Are there adults at the library you have special talks with? _____ Who? _____

r   W   B   C   O   c. Do you have a swimming pool to go to? _____ Whose pool? _____ Are there adults there you have special talks with? _____ Who? _____

r   W   B   C   O   d. Do you go to the grocery store or other kinds of stores? _____ Are there adults at any of these stores with whom you have special talks? _____ Who (which kind of store)? _____

r   W   B   C   O   e. Is there a school yard where you play? _____ Are there adults at the school yard you have special talks with? _____ Who? _____

r   W   B   C   O   f. Is there a park where you play? _____ Are there adults at the park you have special talks with? _____ Who? _____

r   W   B   C   O   g. Where do you play? _____ Are there adults there you have special talks with? _____ Who? _____

W   B   C   O   12. If someone you cared about was having a birthday or other special event, would you be able to go to a store for a present?

_____

r　W　B　C　O　　13. Do you know the names of *all* the people who live next door and across the street from you? Do they talk with you? When was the last time you talked with them?

＿＿＿＿＿＿　＿＿＿＿＿＿

＿＿＿＿＿＿　＿＿＿＿＿＿

＿＿＿＿＿＿　＿＿＿＿＿＿

r　W　B　C　O　　14. a. Do you go visiting with your mother or father? ＿＿＿＿＿＿

b. Where do you go with either or both of them? ＿＿＿＿＿＿

c. To do what (parties, work on projects)? ＿＿＿＿＿＿

　　W　B　C　O　　15. a. Do you play with cousins?

＿＿＿＿＿＿

b. How often? ＿＿＿＿＿＿

AFTER THE WALK

　　W　B　C　O　　16. a. Do you know where your father works? ＿＿＿＿＿＿

b. Do you know his telephone number? ＿＿＿＿＿＿ What is the number? ＿＿＿＿＿＿ If not, do you know where to find it? ＿＿＿＿＿＿

c. Do you know what kind of work your father does? ＿＿＿＿＿＿ What does he do? ＿＿＿＿＿＿

d. Have you been to the place where your father works? ＿＿＿＿＿＿ How often? ＿＿＿＿＿＿

e. Have you seen your father actually working? ＿＿＿＿＿＿

f. Have you helped your father at his work? ＿＿＿＿＿＿

g. If yes, how have you helped?

＿＿＿＿＿＿

　　W　B　C　O　　17. a. Do you know where your mother works? ＿＿＿＿＿＿

b. Do you know her telephone number at work? ＿＿＿＿＿＿ What is the

number? _____ If not, do
you know where to find it?
_____

c. Do you know what kind of work your
mother does? _____

d. Have you been to the place where your
mother works? _____ How
often? _____

e. Have you actually seen your mother
working? _____

f. Have you helped your mother at her
work? _____

g. If yes, how have you helped?
_____

W B C O 18. a. How do you get to school?
_____

b. What do you like about
school? _____

c. Have you received good grades
(honors)? _____ What?
_____

W B C O 19. a. Do you take lessons outside of
school? _____

b. What are they? (dance, music,
acting) _____

c. Are there any other lessons that you
take? (like in school) _____

W B C O 20. a. Do you have any hobbies? (Something
of special interest that you collect or
make or do for fun.) _____
What? _____

b. How do you get your materials?
_____

W B C O 21. a. Do you go to the movies?
_____ How often?
_____

W B C O 22. a. Do you enjoy art and crafts?
_____ Where do you do
them? _____ What do you
like? _____

W B C O 23. a. Does your family own a TV?
_____ Do you watch

TV? _____ How often?
_____ How many programs
each [day/week]? _____ For
how long? _____ What is
your favorite program? _____

b. Do you listen to the radio?
_____ How often?
_____ How many programs
each [day/week]? _____ For
how long? _____ What is
your favorite program? (What do you
listen to?) _____

24. a. Do you read books that adults don't
make you read? _____

b. When was the last time you read a
book? _____

c. What are your favorite books?
_____

25. a. Have you ever had a special part or a
solo in a school band? _____

b. School or church choir? _____

c. School play or program? _____

d. Other? _____

26. a. Some kids your age have make-
believe friends. Do you have one?
_____ What or who is it?
_____

b. Do you have a place you like to pretend
(or fantasize) about running off to?
_____ Where? _____

c. Do you like to pretend (fantasize) that
you are a special person like a rock
singer, a movie star, a doctor or
sports person, or someone else?
_____ Describe _____

27. a. Do you have a pet? _____ If
yes, what kind(s)? _____ Do
you think of your pet as a special
friend? _____ If yes, what
makes [pet] special to you? What do
you like best about [pet]?
_____

b. Are there any neighborhood pets or

animals that you play with?
_____ If yes, do you think of
that pet or animal as a special friend to
you? _____ If yes, what
makes [pet/animal] special to you? What
do you like best about [pet/animal]?

_____

28. Do you have a brother or a sister who
would help you if you needed it?
_____ (like on homework)

29. Do you share a room? _____
(With whom?) _____
(Younger or older?) _____

30. Whom do you like to talk with if you have
something bothering or troubling you?

_____

31. Do you get to use the phone to talk with
friends? _____

32. What do like most about where you
live? _____

33. What do you like least about where you
live? _____

34. Is there something else I should know
about your neighborhood? _____

35. Let's see. We talked about a lot of
different people (and pets and animals)
today who are in your family or in your
life outside your family. Thinking of all
these individuals, who are the most
important to you? First and most
important is who?

	Who?	Age?
1.	_____	_____
2.	_____	_____
3.	_____	_____
4.	_____	_____
5.	_____	_____
6.	_____	_____
7.	_____	_____
8.	_____	_____
9.	_____	_____
10.	_____	_____

36. And for my final questions I again want you to think about all the individuals in your life and tell me:

a. Whom would you go to if you were sad and wanted someone to talk to? _____

b. Whom would you go to if you were angry and wanted someone to talk to? _____

c. Whom would you go to if you were afraid and wanted someone to talk to? _____

d. Whom would you go to if you were really happy and wanted someone to talk to? _____

e. And whom do you share secrets with? _____

ADDENDUM—USED AS NEEDED

CONCEPT	DEFINITION
Relative	For example, someone from your mother's or father's family when they were little (aunts, uncles, cousins, grandparents).
Grandparent generation	People who are older and no longer working.
Honors at school	Some special award or thing you got at school.
Lessons outside school	Classes or lessons in anything.
Hobbies	Something you collect or make or do for fun (anything that is a special interest).
Programs on the radio	What do you listen to?
Least	What you don't like or what you like least of all.

DETAILS OF MEASURES OF SOCIAL-EMOTIONAL FUNCTIONING[6]

I. SOCIAL PERSPECTIVE TAKING SKILL*

Social perspective taking is viewed as the ability to accurately perceive how a situation appears to another person and how that person is reacting cognitively and emotionally (Rothenberg, 1970). As such, it forms the basis for accurately assessing the needs, wishes, and motives of others so that one can respond in a sensitive manner to other persons. This is a skill that is useful in negotiating with peers and adults alike and remains useful throughout the life span. The assumption is that social perspective taking is the ability to understand the affective states of others even though one has not necessarily personally experienced a given event or past. In developing a measure of social perspective taking skill, Rothenberg defined social sensitivity as the ability to accurately perceive and comprehend the behavior, feelings, and motives of other individuals. The Rothenberg (1970) measure consists of four tapes of adult interaction such that the stimuli are as complex as they are in naturalistic conditions and therefore one expressive behavior is not unduly highlighted for the listener. The tapes involve adult rather than child participants to help decrease the likelihood that a child appearing to have social perspective taking ability is actually taking the perspective of another person and not merely attributing characteristics to others that are in fact merely descriptions of himself or herself as experienced in previous situations. The situations were designed to appear realistic but not so commonplace that most children would have had previous experience with identical situations. Four emotions were selected for the central theme: happiness, anger, sadness, and distress or anxiety. Children

---

[6] An asterisk indicates that the measure in question was used in the analyses relating aspects of the Neighborhood Walk to these measures.

are asked to focus primarily on just one of the actors (male or female) in each of the stories. Each tape includes a change in feelings of the main character from initial comments to later ones. After the child listens to a tape, he or she is asked to describe how that actor felt and why he or she felt the way he or she did. To help prevent the possibility of carryover from one story to the next, no two consecutive tape recordings were acted by the same actors. Protocols are scored according to the accuracy in identifying feelings as well as in identifying motives behind the feelings.

Rothenberg (1970) developed this measure with 108 third- and fifth-grade children. Rothenberg obtained interrater reliability for each of the four tapes ranging from $r = .86$ to $r = .96$. Internal consistency was considered by the intercorrelations between the four tapes and ranged between $r = .28$ and $r = .47$. While these correlations are not sufficiently high to say that all four tapes are measuring exactly the same thing, they are high enough to justify pooling the scores of each tape into one measure of social perspective taking ability.

With respect to validity, fifth graders demonstrated greater social perspective taking skill than did third graders. Social perspective taking skill was also positively correlated with measures of intelligence. Furthermore, children rated by peers as low in interpersonal adjustment obtained significantly lower scores on the tapes assumed to be more stressful (anger, sadness, anxiety) than did the well-adjusted children. Likewise, children rated as low in interpersonal adjustment did more poorly on the stressful tapes than did well-adjusted children.

II. TOLERANCE FOR AMBIGUITY IN INTERPERSONAL SITUATIONS

"An ambiguous situation may be defined as one which cannot be adequately structured or categorized by the individual because of lack of sufficient cues" (Budner, 1962, p. 30). Interest in tolerance of ambiguity among children derives chiefly from the work of Frenkel-Brunswik (1949), who attempted to relate intolerance of ambiguity to ethnocentrism, and more recently from the work of Harrington, Block, and Block (1978) relating tolerance of ambiguity to behavior in relatively unstructured situations. Functional relationships involving intolerance of ambiguity and anxiety have been demonstrated for children aged 10–14 (Smock, 1957, 1958) as well as for younger children (Harrington et al., 1978).

The paper-and-pencil measure developed for and prior to the present study was designed to measure how flexible the child is in evaluating a social situation. A sample item taken from the measure is, "A kid comes up and slugs you." What are the possibilities of why this happened?

a) because he's mad at you;
b) because he's upset with an older brother; or
c) because he's upset with a younger brother.

Clearly, all three responses are possible reasons why one child might hit another. This measure consists of 20 items, with some items having all three choices as feasible rationale and other items having just one or two feasible reasons. Based on the sample of 108 fourth graders, test-retest data (across a 2-week interval) yielded adequate reliability for this measure of tolerance for ambiguity in interpersonal situations. Test-retest reliability was $r = .81$. No significant relationship was found between tolerance for ambiguity and Crandall, Crandall, and Katkovsky's (1965) measure of social desirability.

III. LOCUS OF CONTROL ORIENTATION*

If a person perceives that an event is contingent on his or her own behavior or his or her own relatively permanent characteristics, this person is considered to have an internal control orientation. Nowicki and his associates (Nowicki & Duke, 1974; Nowicki & Strickland, 1973) have developed a series of scales to assess across a wide age range children's generalized internal-external locus of control orientation.

The Preschool and Primary Nowicki-Strickland Internal-External control scale consists of 26 items. Six-week test-retest reliability for the 7-year-olds on this measure was $r(59) = .79$, $p < .001$. The relationship between this scale and social desirability was found to be nonsignificant. S. Nowicki and M. Duke (personal communication, 1973), using a sample of 600 children ranging in age from 4 to 9, found internal consistency estimates ranging from $r = .66$ to $r = .79$. Validity evidence is based on significant relations obtained with measures of achievement and popularity as well as a highly significant relation ($r = .88$) to the Nowicki and Strickland childhood measures of locus of control (S. Nowicki and M. Duke, personal communication, 1973).

With respect to the 40-item Nowicki-Strickland locus of control scale for children (Nowicki & Strickland, 1973), test-retest reliability obtained from group administration of the measure (6 weeks apart) was $r = .63$ for a sample of third-, fourth-, and fifth-grade children. An estimate of the internal consistency corrected by the Spearman-Brown formula was $r = .63$ also. No significant relationship was found between locus of control and social desirability. Nowicki and Strickland report moderate correlations between the children's locus of control scale (Nowicki & Strickland, 1973), the Intellectual Achievement Responsibility scale ($r = .31$ for third graders), and the Bialer-Cromwell scale ($r = .41$ for a sample aged 9–11). Other correlates of internality include a positive relationship to popularity (Nowicki, 1971; Nowicki & Barnes, 1973) and a negative relationship to prejudice against Negroes (Nowicki & Strickland, 1973).

IV. TOLERANCE FOR AMBIVALENCE OF FEELINGS

Having access to the full range of affective responses, including seemingly contradictory and at times "ungrateful/selfish" emotional reactions, can be viewed in clinical terms as a healthy state of affairs. Although a tolerance for ambivalence of feelings is a common clinical issue, there is no empirical tradition for studying this phenomenon. The present measure of tolerance for ambivalence of feelings was developed for and prior to the present study; it consists of 20 items and was designed to measure the child's comfort in recognizing and accepting his or her conflicting feelings, specifically, the child's tendency to accept or reject ambivalent feelings. Out of 20 items, 10 give cues to indicate a basis for an ambivalent response. A sample ambivalence item from this measure is, "You told your parents what you want for your birthday. They give you a really super gift, but it wasn't what you asked for . . ."

  a) You are disappointed that you didn't get what you were
       hoping for.
  b) You are pleased with the gift you got.
  c) You are both disappointed and pleased with the gift.

Scores on this measure are based on these "ambivalence items." The other 10 items are "filler" items and include descriptions of situations with cues to only a single affective response. A sample filler item is, "One day when you're at the department store with your mother, you see a toddler standing alone in an aisle crying and crying. A disgusted saleslady walks right past the child saying, 'I wish these parents would keep track of their bratty kids.' The child continues to cry and no one tries to find the mother . . ."

  a) It makes you sad to see this little kid lost and crying.
  b) You're pleased the saleslady appears so sympathetic.
  c) You feel both sad and pleased about the situation.

Based on a sample of 108 fourth graders, test-retest data (across a 2-week interval) yielded adequate reliability for this measure of tolerance for ambivalence of feelings. Test-retest reliability was $r = .81$. Scores on this measure were also found to be negatively related to Crandall et al.'s (1965) measure of social desirability, $r(54) = -.35$, $p < .001$. Thus responding in a socially desirable response set is related to low tolerance for ambivalence of feelings.

V. ATTITUDES TOWARD COMPETITION*

VI. ATTITUDES TOWARD COOPERATION

VII. ATTITUDES TOWARD INDIVIDUALISM*

These three scales were taken from the Minnesota School Affect Assessment (MSAA) procedure developed by Ahlgren et al. (1977). The MSAA was designed to assess pupils' feelings toward many facets of their schooling experience. The competition, cooperation, and individualism scores each consist of the sum of three true-false items. An example from the competition scale is, "I like to get better marks than other students do"; an example from the cooperation scale is, "I like to learn by working together with other students"; and an example from the individualism scale is, "I like to work by myself in school." Internal consistency was calculated on the basis of the Cronbach alpha coefficient for the cluster scores and was found to be .82 for the competition scale, .72 for the cooperation scale, and .74 for the individualism scale (Ahlgren et al., 1977). Attitude toward cooperation was consistently related to a broad range of positive attitudes toward schooling at all grade levels (Johnson & Ahlgren, 1976). Johnson and Ahlgren also found that competitiveness changed its pattern of correlates, showing relationships to several positive attitudes only in high school but showing no such relationships during the elementary school years.

VIII. EMPATHY*

Empathy refers to the vicarious emotional response to the perceived emotional experience of others, and the emphasis is on emotional responsiveness rather than on accuracy of cognitive social insight (Bryant, 1982). The scale consists of 22 items with a yes/no (me/not me) format. The total score on the measure is the sum of the items answered in the empathic direction. Test-retest reliability coefficients were .74 for first graders and .81 for fourth graders. Bryant further documented a basis for construct validity of this measure of empathy. The empathy index demonstrated significant relations to aggressiveness among first- and fourth-grade boys and significant relations to acceptance of individual differences for each of these age groups as well. Thus scores on this measure of empathy are related to the expression of social behavior of children in middle childhood. Empathy scores have also been found to predict the current social adjustment of girls during middle childhood and are predictive of limited aspects of mental health during early adolescence (Bryant, 1984). The index was not significantly correlated with social desirability or reading achievement (Bryant, 1982).

IX. ACCEPTANCE OF HELP

Wright (1960) argues that dependency behaviors are critical in establishing and maintaining many important kinds of satisfying interpersonal relations. There are times when it is useful to be able to rely on others, to ask for and accept help. She argues that dependence is not necessarily a second-best alternative but a valuable end in itself. Wright suggests researchers have arbitrarily, due to cultural biases, ignored the need for being comfortable with aspects of dependency in interpersonal relations throughout the life span. Acceptance of help (Maccoby, 1961) is intended to tap the child's comfort with emotional sharing and readiness to rely on others. A measure of acceptance of dependency needs was, thus, considered important to include as an aspect of psychological well-being. The measure in the present study combines accepting material help as well as accepting comfort (Maccoby, 1961) and consists of eight items. Maccoby's initial work with this measure was done with sixth graders, and actual scores of reliability were not recorded. Internal consistency, based on the Cronbach alpha, was calculated for the present sample. The Cronbach alpha was .51 for the 7-year-olds, .40 for the 10-year-olds, and .46 for the total sample; while these scores are not sufficiently high to say that all items measure exactly the same thing, they are high enough to justify pooling the items into a single score of general acceptance of help.

X. SELF-EVALUATION

This measure was designed to assess how children evaluate three different aspects of their development relative to peers (Zingale et al., 1978). The three aspects of development were the amount of positive internal experiences (i.e., fun), school performance, and social relations. For example, children were asked, "Do you feel youngsters your age have: a) more fun? b) less fun? c) about the same?" In other words, children assessed their capacities in relation to their peers. This scale is in its developmental phases with no reported reliability or validity. The multidimensional nature of this measure is reflected in its Cronbach alpha of .61 for the 7-year-olds and .42 for the 10-year-olds in the present study.

XI. ACCEPTANCE OF INDIVIDUAL DIFFERENCES*

This measure was designed to assess the physical closeness a child will allow a wide variety of children, including children that have been shown to be negatively evaluated by groups of children (Bryant, 1982): those who do not do well in school (are "dumb") or are overweight ("fat") (Roff, Sell, & Golden, 1972); those who are racially different (Koslin, Amarel, & Ames, 1970; Powell & White, 1969; Seeman, 1946); and those who are learning disabled (Bryan, 1976), "emotionally disturbed" (Novak, 1974), or physically unattractive (Kleck, Richardson, & Ronald, 1974; Roff et al., 1972). Specifically, children were asked to mark on each of eight lines emanating from a common point how close they want each of eight variously described children to come to them: "The child will stop where you decide you would feel uncomfortable with the child's closeness to you." The children responding consider themselves standing at the central point. This procedure comes from the comfortable interpersonal distance (CID) measure reported by Duke and Nowicki (1972). To establish a frame of reference, the first judgment is made with respect to one's best friend. Then, following Novak's script, the description of each imaginary child begins with: "This is a boy/girl your age and in the same grade as you. He/she has some hobbies and also enjoys watching TV" (1974, p. 462). This brief introduction is intended to identify each child as a member of the "human race." Subsequent descriptions refer to the following types of children: depressed, immature, aggressive, schizoid, and normal (Novak, 1974) and also overweight and academically low. Females were presented with descriptions of girls, and males were presented with descriptions of boys. The instructions for the first graders were modified according to Duke and Wilson's (1973) adaptation of the CID for preschool children (using dolls that children move rather than making pencil marks). Scores are the sum of the distances from the center of each mark.

Duke and Nowicki (1972) report that the CID is not related to social desirability (Crandall et al., 1965) response style. Validity for the CID is based on correlations of CID scores with the actual approach behavior of adults (Johnson, 1972; and Martin, 1972; both are cited in Duke & Nowicki, 1972). Among other additional sources of validity, Duke and Nowicki (1972) present data from comfortable interpersonal distance judgments that supported predictions based on previously documented relationships: children and adults maintained a greater distance from persons of a different race;

prepubescent children preferred that opposite-sex persons keep further away than same-sex individuals; and the more a person liked someone, the closer the chosen interpersonal distance.

Test-retest data (across a 2-week interval) yielded adequate reliability for this acceptance of individual differences measure (Bryant, 1982). Among first graders test-retest reliability was $r(53) = .75$, $p < .001$, and among fourth graders reliability was $r(106) = .86$, $p < .001$. In addition, no relation between Crandall et al.'s (1965) social desirability and acceptance of individual differences has been found.

APPENDIX D

TABLE D1

DESCRIPTIVE STATISTICS FOR MEASURES OF SOCIAL-EMOTIONAL FUNCTIONING

MEASURE	7-YEAR-OLDS ($N = 72$)			10-YEAR-OLDS ($N = 96$)			TOTAL SAMPLE ($N = 168$)		
	M	SD	Obtained Range	M	SD	Obtained Range	M	SD	Obtained Range
Social perspective taking ...	9.32	4.13	−2–18	18.56	6.27	8–38	14.60	7.12	−2–38
Tolerance for ambiguity ...	...	...	...	24.66	6.15	14–36	...	...	...
Locus of control (z score)...	.00	.99	−2.49–2.27	.00	1.00	−2.42–2.20	.00	.99	−2.49–2.27
Tolerance for ambivalence	...	...	...	5.23	2.58	0–10	...	...	...
Attitudes toward competition ...	5.78	2.56	0–9	6.16	2.34	0–9	5.99	2.44	0–9
Attitudes toward cooperation ...	6.11	2.76	0–9	6.48	1.49	2–9	6.32	2.13	0–9
Attitudes toward individualism ...	5.08	2.59	0–9	4.63	2.18	0–9	4.82	2.37	0–9
Empathy ...	12.82	2.79	6–20	13.87	3.16	5–20	13.42	3.04	5–20
Acceptance of help ...	5.58	1.69	1–8	5.51	1.59	1–8	5.54	1.64	1–8
Self-evaluation ...	4.15	1.13	1–7	4.05	1.40	1–7	4.11	1.27	1–7
Acceptance of individual differences ...	343.26	88.58	146–572	316.85	78.73	141–514	328.17	83.87	141–572

NEIGHBORHOOD WALK CATEGORIES OF REPORTED SOURCES OF SUPPORT

CATEGORY	DEFINITION
OTHERS AS SOURCES OF SUPPORT	
1. Know and interact with peer generation	Child has friends (one point); child has a best friend (one point); number of friend's homes child can knock on door; child visits cousins frequently (e.g., daily or weekly) (two points) or infrequently (one point); child has a sibling who would help if help were needed (one point).
2. Know and interact with adult generation	Number of adults child knows in the neighborhood; number of nearby adult neighbors child talks to.
3. Know and interact with grandparent generation	Number of adults child visits who are older and no longer working; multiply two times the number of grandparent sets that child visits frequently (daily or weekly); number of grandparent sets that child visits infrequently; number of grandparents child lives with.
4. Intimate talks with peer generation	Number of times peers identified as resource to whom child goes for intimate talks when child is

5. Intimate talks with parent generation — Number of times parent-generation adults identified as resource for intimate talks.

6. Intimate talks with grandparent generation — Number of times grandparent-generation adults identified as resource for intimate talks.

7. Intimate talks with pet "generation" — Number of times pets identified as resource for intimate talks.

8. Peer generation among 10 most important individuals — Number of peers child includes in a list of 10 most important individuals.

9. Parent generation among 10 most important individuals — Number of parent-generation adults child includes in a list of 10 most important individuals.

10. Grandparent generation among 10 most important individuals — Number of grandparent-generation adults child includes in a list of 10 most important individuals.

11. Pet generation among 10 most important individuals — Number of pets child includes in a list of 10 most important individuals.

12. Pets as special friends — Number of different kinds of family pets child considers as special friends; number of different kinds of neighborhood pets child considers as special friends.

13. Special talks with adults — Number of adults child has special talks with at church, at libraries, at pools, at stores, at school yards, at parks, at places child plays; number of teachers child enjoys talking with outside class.

14. Involvement in father's work — Child knows where father works (one point); child knows father's phone number at work (two points) or knows how to look it up (one point); child visits father's work frequently (i.e., daily or weekly) (two points) or infrequently (one point); child has seen father

(beginning) bothered, sad, angry, or happy and to share secrets.

99

15. Involvement in mother's work

working (one point); child helps father at work (two points). Child knows where mother works (one point); child knows mother's phone number at work (two points) or knows how to look it up (one point); child visits mother's work frequently (e.g., daily or weekly) (two points) or infrequently (one point); child has seen mother working (one point); child helps mother at work (two points).

INTRAPERSONAL SOURCES OF SUPPORT

1. Fantasies (unstructured)

Number of make-believe friends child has; number of places child pretends about running off to; number of special people child pretends to be.

2. Fantasies (structured)

Number of hours per day child watches television; number of hours per day child listens to radio.

3. Hobbies

Number of different kinds of hobbies child reports; number of different kinds of arts and crafts child likes to do.

4. Skill development and expression

Number of things child likes about school; child has received good grades (one point); number of honors child has received; number of different kinds of lessons child takes outside school; number of different kinds of lessons child takes in school; number of special parts or solos child has had in school band, in school or church choir, in school play or program, or in church or community play or program; child has read a book within the last week (one point).

ENVIRONMENTAL SOURCES OF SUPPORT

1. Places to get off to by self

Child has a special place to be alone (one point); child could go to the store for a present (one point); child allowed to use the telephone by self or on own initiative every day (one point).

2. Formally sponsored organizations (structured)

Number of organizations child belongs to; child goes to church or temple (one point); child attends parties after church or temple services (one point).

3. Formally sponsored organizations (unstructured)

Number of libraries child uses; number of community pools child goes to; number of club pools child goes to; number of parks where child plays; child plays at community facilities (one point); number of school yards where child plays.

4. Informal, unsponsored meeting places

Number of friends' homes in which child can play inside; child goes to a relative's pool (one point); child goes to a nonrelative's pool (one point); number of neighborhood clubs child belongs to.

TABLE F1

MEANS, STANDARD DEVIATIONS, AND OBTAINED RANGES OF SUPPORT CATEGORIES

	Overall			Males		Females		7-Year-Olds		10-Year-Olds		Small Families		Large Families	
	M	SD	Obtained Range	M	SD	M	SD	M	SD	M	SD	M	SD	M	SD
Others as sources of support:															
Know and interact with peers	9.19	4.05	3–25	9.67	4.81	8.71	3.06	…	…	…	…	8.87	4.20	10.66	4.01
Know and interact with adult generation	4.61	2.36	0–14	5.08	2.38	4.14	2.26	…	…	…	…	…	…	…	…
Know and interact with grandparent generation	2.52	1.54	0–7	…	…	…	…	…	…	…	…	…	…	…	…
Intimate talks with peers	2.70	1.91	0–11	2.30	1.60	3.11	2.11	…	…	…	…	…	…	…	…
Intimate talks with parent generation	4.00	2.42	0–11	4.27	2.36	3.73	2.46	…	…	…	…	4.40	2.29	3.59	2.46
Intimate talks with grandparent generation	.07	.36	0–3	…	…	…	…	…	…	.11	.46	.01	.11	.13	.49
Intimate talks with pets	.22	.68	0–4	.13	.43	.31	.85	.01	.12	…	…	…	…	…	…
Peers among 10 most important individuals	4.51	2.46	0–10	…	…	…	…	4.97	2.49	4.16	2.39	4.01	2.40	5.01	2.42
Parent generation among 10 most important individuals	2.97	1.72	0–10	…	…	…	…	2.64	1.63	3.21	1.75	…	…	…	…
Grandparent generation among 10 most important individuals	1.27	1.45	0–5	…	…	…	…	1.01	1.37	1.46	1.48	…	…	…	…
Pets among 10 most important individuals	1.00	1.49	0–6	…	…	…	…	…	…	…	…	…	…	…	…
Pets as special friends	1.72	1.03	0–4	1.56	1.06	1.88	.97	1.50	.99	1.89	1.02	…	…	…	…
Special talks with adults	2.38	2.23	0–13	…	…	…	…	…	…	…	…	…	…	…	…
Involvement in father's work	4.10	1.93	0–8	…	…	…	…	3.72	1.95	4.39	1.88	…	…	…	…
Involvement in mother's work	5.51	2.48	0–8	…	…	…	…	…	…	…	…	…	…	…	…
Intrapersonal sources of support:															
Fantasies (unstructured)	1.64	1.40	0–8	…	…	…	…	…	…	…	…	…	…	…	…
Fantasies (structured)	4.38	2.88	0–17	4.05	2.63	4.70	3.09	…	…	…	…	…	…	…	…
Hobbies	2.34	1.02	0–7	2.18	1.03	2.50	.99	…	…	…	…	…	…	…	…
Skill development and expression	6.01	2.63	0–17	…	…	…	…	4.78	1.75	6.93	2.80	…	…	…	…
Environmental sources of support:															
Places to get off to by self	2.15	.58	1–4	…	…	…	…	2.06	.60	2.22	.55	…	…	…	…
Formally sponsored organizations (structured)	1.64	1.15	0–5	…	…	…	…	1.25	.96	1.93	1.19	…	…	…	…
Formally sponsored organizations (unstructured)	2.89	.99	0–5	…	…	…	…	…	…	…	…	…	…	…	…
Informal, unsponsored meeting places	5.54	3.89	0–25	…	…	…	…	…	…	…	…	…	…	…	…

TABLE G1

MEANS AND STANDARD DEVIATIONS ACCORDING TO AGE AND SEX OF RESPONDENT
FOR SELECTED MEASURES OF SOCIAL-EMOTIONAL FUNCTIONING

| | 7-YEAR-OLDS | | | | 10-YEAR-OLDS | | | |
| | Males | | Females | | Males | | Females | |
	M	SD	M	SD	M	SD	M	SD
Empathy	12.11	2.58	13.53	2.84	12.80	2.90	14.94	3.08
Acceptance of individual differences ...	364.67	93.39	321.86	80.25	321.85	79.71	311.85	78.27
Attitudes toward competition ...	5.61	2.59	5.94	2.56	7.06	1.20	5.25	2.33
Social perspective taking	8.83	4.45	9.81	3.78	17.94	6.05	19.19	6.50

TABLE H1

SELECTED NETWORK OF SUPPORT FOR PREDICTING EMPATHY—REDUCED MODEL

Predictor Variables	Beta	$F(1,152)$	p
Control variables:[a]			
Sex of child	−.43	9.35	.01
Age	.19	.70	...
Family size	−.33	5.72	.05
Sex of sibling	−.09	1.78	...
SES	−.11	2.71	...
Intimate talks with pets	.02	.07	...
Know and interact with parent generation	.02	.08	...
Know and interact with grandparent generation	−.12	2.88	...
Grandparent generation among 10 most important individuals	.14	3.93	.05
Selected variables:[b]			
Intimate talks with pets × age	.17	5.45	.05
Know and interact with parent generation × family size	.35	5.49	.05
Know and interact with grandparent generation × sex of child	.33	6.44	.05
Grandparent generation among 10 most important individuals × sex of child	−.22	5.56	.05
Intimate talks with grandparent generation	−.25	2.28	...
Intimate talks with grandparent generation × family size	.43	6.93	.01

[a] $R_{control} = .41$.
[b] $pR_{select} = .44$, $F(6,152) = 6.16$, $p < .001$; $R_{total} = .57$, $F(15,152) = 5.00$, $p < .001$.

TABLE H2

SELECTED NETWORK OF SUPPORT FOR PREDICTING ACCEPTANCE OF INDIVIDUAL
DIFFERENCES—REDUCED MODEL

Predictor Variables	Beta	$F(1,151)$	p
Control variables:[a]			
Sex of child	.15	3.75	...
Age	.32	2.83	...
Family size	−.71	4.72	.05
Sex of sibling	.13	2.96	...
SES	−.05	.31	...
Sex × age	−.05	.40	...
Intimate talks with pets	.09	.82	...
Intimate talks with pets × age	−.22	4.65	.05
Intimate talks with pets × sex of child	.08	.62	...
Informal, unsponsored meeting places	.02	.08	...
Places to get off to by self	−.04	.28	...
Involvement in mother's work	.11	1.95	...
Selected support variables:[b]			
Intimate talks with pets × sex of child × age	−.18	3.20	.08
Informal, unsponsored meeting places × family size	.27	4.05	.05
Places to get off to by self × family size	.58	3.69	.06
Involvement with mother's work × age	−.47	5.93	.05

[a] $R_{control} = .34$.

[b] $pR_{select} = .33$, $F(4,151) = 4.49$, $p < .001$; $R_{total} = .46$, $F(16,151) = 2.51$, $p < .001$.

TABLE H3

SELECTED NETWORK OF SUPPORT FOR PREDICTING ATTITUDES TOWARD
COMPETITION—REDUCED MODEL

Predictor Variables	Beta	$F(1,152)$	p
Control variables:[a]			
Sex of child	−.10	.55	...
Age	.25	2.15	...
Family size	−.03	.16	...
Sex of sibling	.15	4.45	.05
SES	.07	.95	...
Sex × age	.53	15.51	.001
Intimate talks with pets	−.05	.42	...
Pets as special friends	.05	.46	...
Informal, unsponsored meeting places	−.08	.93	...
Informal, unsponsored meeting places × sex of child	.31	4.95	.05
Informal, unsponsored meeting places × age	−.02	.02	...
Selected support variables:[b]			
Intimate talks with pets × age	.24	8.50	.01
Intimate talks with pets × family size	−.17	4.00	.05
Pets as special friends × age	−.22	2.12	...
Informal, unsponsored meeting places × sex of child × age	−.39	7.94	.01

[a] $R_{control} = .38$.

[b] $pR_{select} = .34$, $F(4,152) = 4.97$, $p < .001$; $R_{total} = .49$, $F(15,152) = 3.26$, $p < .001$.

TABLE H4

Selected Network of Support for Predicting Social Perspective Taking—Reduced Model

Predictor Variables	Beta	$F(1,152)$	p
Control variable:[a]			
Sex of child	−.40	8.89	.01
Age	.27	2.62	...
Family size	−.01	.08	...
Sex of sibling	−.04	.55	...
SES	−.26	21.16	.001
Know and interact with parent generation	−.08	1.91	...
Know and interact with grandparent generation	.08	2.26	...
Intimate talks with grandparent generation	−.06	.89	...
Formally sponsored organizations—unstructured activities	.04	.46	...
Selected support variables:[b]			
Hobbies	.10	3.40	.07
Skill development and expression	.12	3.91	.05
Know and interact with parent generation × sex of child	.23	3.74	.06
Know and interact with grandparent generation × sex of child	.17	2.80	.10
Intimate talks with grandparent generation × sex of child	.13	4.59	.05
Formally sponsored organizations—unstructured activities × age	.34	4.12	.05

[a] $R_{control} = .38$.
[b] $pR_{select} = .44$, $F(6,152) = 5.90$, $p < .001$; $R_{total} = .78$, $F(15,152) = 15.48$, $p < .001$.

TABLE H5

Selected Network of Support for Predicting Attitudes toward Individualism—Reduced Model

Predictor Variables	Beta	$F(1,154)$	p
Control variables:[a]			
Sex of child	.07	.83	...
Age	.22	2.42	...
Family size	.60	4.78	.05
Sex of sibling	.07	.81	...
SES	−.04	.25	...
Intimate talks with peer generation	−.01	.02	...
Formally sponsored organizations—unstructured activities	.08	.95	...
Formally sponsored organizations—structured activities	−.01	.018	...
Informal, unsponsored meeting places	.09	1.41	...
Selected support variables:[b]			
Intimate talks with peer generation × age	−.41	9.22	.01
Formally sponsored organizations—unstructured activities × family size	−.59	5.92	.05
Formally sponsored organizations—structured activities × family size	−.26	3.64	...
Informal, unsponsored meeting places × family size	.25	3.40	...

[a] $R_{control} = .15$.
[b] $pR_{select} = .36$, $F(4,154) = 5.67$, $p < .001$; $R_{total} = .39$, $F(13,154) = 2.06$, $p < .05$.

TABLE H6

Selected Network of Support for Predicting Locus of Control (z Score)—Reduced Model

Predictor Variables	Beta	$F(1,151)$	p
Control variables:[a]			
Sex of child	−.13	.48	...
Age	.04	.06	...
Family size	−.14	2.20	...
Sex of sibling	.02	.12	...
SES	−.33	19.69	.001
Sex of child × age	−.18	1.58	...
Know and interact with parent generation	.02	.10	...
Special talks with parent generation	−.16	4.17	.05
Grandparent generation among 10 most important individuals	.02	.04	...
Know and interact with grandparent generation	.02	.04	...
Know and interact with grandparent generation × sex of child	−.03	.03	...
Know and interact with grandparent generation × age	−.06	.17	...
Selected support variables:[b]			
Know and interact with parent generation × sex	.42	6.38	.05
Special talks with parent generation × sex	−.24	4.25	.05
Grandparent generation among 10 most important individuals × family size	.33	11.03	.001
Know and interact with grandparent generation × sex of child × age	.25	2.89	...

[a] $R_{control} = .35$.
[b] $pR_{select} = .37$, $F(4,151) = 6.01$, $p < .001$; $R_{total} = .49$, $F(16,151) = 3.02$, $p < .001$.

TABLE I1

DESCRIPTIVE DATA FOR THE ACCESSIBILITY SCORES

ACCESSIBILITY MEASURE	7-YEAR-OLDS		10-YEAR-OLDS		OBTAINED RANGE
	M	SD	M	SD	
Access to grandparent generation	.26	.53	.33	.52	0–2
Access to special talks with adults	.68	.87	.72	1.01	0–4
Access to hobbies	1.72	1.06	1.91	1.17	0–4
Access to skill development and expression ..	.76	.68	1.23	.84	0–3
Access to places to get off by oneself	.60	.64	1.08	.68	0–2
Access to formally sponsored organizations—structured activities	.13	.33	.53	.95	0–5
Access to formally sponsored organizations—unstructured activities	1.06	.87	1.51	.92	0–3

REFERENCES

Achenbach, T. M., & Edelbrock, C. S. (1978). The classification of child psychopathology: A review and analysis of empirical efforts. *Psychological Bulletin, 85*(6), 1275–1301.

Achenbach, T. M., & Edelbrock, C. S. (1981). Behavioral problems and competencies reported by parents of normal and disturbed children aged four through sixteen. *Monographs of the Society for Research in Child Development, 46*(1, Serial No. 188).

Advisory Committee on Child Development. (1976). *Toward a national policy for children and families.* Washington, DC: National Academy of Science.

Ahlgren, A., Christensen, D. J., & Lum, K. (1977). *Minnesota school affect assessments.* Minneapolis: University of Minnesota.

Ainsworth, M. D. (1967). *Infancy in Uganda: Infant care and the growth of love.* Baltimore: Johns Hopkins University Press.

Barker, R. G., & Wright, H. F. (1951). *One boy's day.* New York: Harper & Row.

Baumrind, D. (1975). Early socialization in adolescent competence. In S. E. Dragastin & G. Elder, Jr. (Eds.), *Adolescence in the life cycle* (pp. 117–143). Washington, DC: Hemisphere.

Belle, D., & Longfellow, C. (1983, April). [Untitled presentation]. In S. Crockenberg (Chair), *Social support, parenting and child development.* Symposium conducted at the biennial meeting of the Society for Research in Child Development, Detroit. (From *Society for Research in Child Development: Abstracts from the biennial meeting, 50th anniversary, 1933–1983,* 1983, **4,** 340)

Bem, S. (1975). Sex role adaptability: One consequence of psychological androgyny. *Journal of Personality and Social Psychology, 31,* 634–643.

Berndt, T. J. (1981). *Prosocial behavior between friends and the development of social interaction patterns.* Paper presented at the biennial meeting of the Society for Research in Child Development, Boston.

Blyth, D. A. (1982). Mapping the social world of adolescents: Issues, techniques, and problems. In F. Serafica (Ed.), *Social cognition, context, and social behavior: A developmental perspective.* New York: Guilford Press.

Blyth, D. A., Hill, J. P., & Thiel, K. S. (1982). Early adolescents' significant others: Grade and gender differences with familial and non-familial adults and young people. *Journal of Youth and Adolescence, 11*(6), 425–450.

Bossard, J. H. S., & Boll, E. S. (1956). *The large family system.* Philadelphia: University of Pennsylvania Press.

Bradburn, N. (1969). *The structure of psychological well-being.* Chicago: Aldine.

Brim, O. G. (1975). Macro-structural influences on child development and the need for childhood social indicators. *American Journal of Orthopsychiatry, 45*(4), 516–524.

Brim, O. G., White, K. L., & Zill, N. (1978). *Child trends international: A plan for an organiza-*

tion to improve the quality, scope and use of information about children. Unpublished manuscript.

Bronfenbrenner, U. (1972). *Two worlds of childhood: U.S. and U.S.S.R.* New York: Russell Sage.

Bronfenbrenner, U. (1977). Toward an experimental ecology of human development. *American Psychologist, 32,* 513–531.

Bronfenbrenner, U. (1979). *The ecology of human development: Experiments by nature and design.* Cambridge, MA: Harvard University Press.

Bryan, T. H. (1976). Peer popularity of learning disabled children: A replication. *Journal of Learning Disabilities, 9*(5), 307–311.

Bryant, B. K. (1982). An index of empathy for children and adolescents. *Child Development, 53,* 413–425.

Bryant, B. K. (1984, August). Self-criticism of the Bryant (1982) empathy index. In R. Lennon (Chair), *The construct and assessment of empathy.* Symposium conducted at the annual meeting of the American Psychological Association, Toronto.

Budner, S. (1962). Intolerance of ambiguity as a personality variable. *Journal of Personality, 30,* 29–50.

Campbell, A. (1981). *The sense of well-being in America.* New York: McGraw-Hill.

Caplan, G. (1974). *Support systems and community mental health.* New York: Behavioral Publications.

Caplan, G., & Grunebaum, H. (1967). Perspective on primary prevention: A review. *Archives of General Psychiatry, 17,* 331–346.

Coates, G., & Bussard, E. (1974). Patterns of children's spatial behavior in a moderate-density housing development. In D. H. Carson (Ed.), *Man-environment interactions: Evaluations and applications* (Pt. 3, pp. 131–142). New York: Wiley.

Cochran, M., & Brassard, J. A. (1979). Child development and personal social networks. *Child Development, 50,* 601–616.

Cohen, T., & Cohen, P. (1975). *Applied multiple regression/correlation analysis for the behavioral sciences.* New York: Erlbaum.

Conger, J. J. (1981). Freedom and commitment: Families, youth, and social change. *American Psychologist, 36*(2), 1475–1484.

Crandall, V. C., Crandall, V. J., & Katkovsky, W. (1965). A children's social desirability questionnaire. *Journal of Consulting Psychology, 29*(1), 27–36.

Dabrowski, K. (1964). *Positive disintegration.* Boston: Little, Brown.

Duke, M. P., & Nowicki, S. (1972). A new measure and social-learning model for interpersonal distance. *Journal of Experimental Research in Personality, 6,* 119–132.

Duke, M. P., & Wilson, J. (1973). A note on the measurement of interpersonal distance in preschool children. *Journal of Genetic Psychology, 123,* 361–362.

Elder, G. H. (1974). *Children of the Great Depression.* Chicago: University of Chicago Press.

Erikson, E. H. (1950). *Childhood and society.* New York: Norton.

Erikson, E. H. (1964). *Insight and responsibility: Lectures on the ethical implications of psychoanalytic insight.* New York: Norton.

Fischer, C. S., Jackson, R. M., Stueve, C. A., Gerson, K., Jones, L. M., & Baldassari, M. (1977). *Networks and places: Social relations in the urban setting.* New York: Free Press.

Frenkel-Brunswik, E. (1949). Intolerance of ambiguity as an emotional and perceptual personality variable. *Journal of Personality, 18,* 108–143.

Freud, S. (1953). Three essays on sexuality. In J. Strachey (Ed. and Trans.), *The standard edition of the complete psychological works of Sigmund Freud* (Vol. 7, pp. 125–245). London: Hogarth.

Garbarino, J., Burston, N., Raber, S., Russell, R., & Crouter, A. (1978). The social maps of children approaching adolescence: Studying the ecology of youth development. *Journal of Youth and Adolescence, 7*(4), 417–428.

Garbarino, J., & Gilliam, G. (1980). *Understanding abusive families.* Lexington, MA: Lexington Books.

Garmezy, N. (1982). Foreword. In E. Werner & R. Smith, *Vulnerable but invincible: A longitudinal study of resilient children and youth.* Monterey, CA: Brooks/Cole.

Giovannoni, J. M., & Billingsley, A. (1970). Child neglect among the poor: A study of parental adequacy in families of three ethnic groups. *Child Welfare, 49,* 196–204.

Gottschalk, L. A. (1974). A hope scale applicable to verbal samples. *Archives of General Psychiatry, 30,* 779–785.

Hagestad, G. O., & Speicher, J. L. (1981). *Grandparents and family influence: Views of three generations.* Paper presented at the biennial meeting of the Society for Research in Child Development, Boston.

Hamburg, D. A., & Adams, J. E. (1967). A perspective on coping behavior: Seeking and utilizing information in major transitions. *Archives of General Psychiatry, 17,* 277–284.

Harrington, D. M., Block, J. H., & Block, J. (1978). Intolerance of ambiguity in preschool children: Psychometric considerations, behavioral manifestations, and parental correlates. *Developmental Psychology, 14*(3), 242–256.

Hart, R. (1978). *Children's sense of place.* New York: Halstead.

Himmelweit, H. T., Oppenheim, A. N., & Vince, P. (1958). *Television and the child.* London: Oxford University Press.

Hoffman, L. (1979). Maternal employment: 1979. *American Psychologist, 34*(10), 859–865.

Hollingshead, A. (1965). *Two factor index of social position.* New Haven, CT: Yale Station.

Jersild, A. J. (1947). *Child psychology.* London: Straple.

Johnson, D. W., & Ahlgren, A. (1976). Relationship between student attitudes about cooperation and competition and attitudes toward schooling. *Journal of Educational Psychology, 68,* 92–102.

Johnson, D. W., & Norem-Hebeisen, A. A. (1979). A measure of cooperative, competitive, and individualistic attitudes. *Journal of Social Psychology, 109,* 253–261.

Johnson, I. (1972). *Interpersonal distancing responses of black versus white females.* Paper presented at Southeastern Psychological Association meeting, Atlanta, GA.

Kerlinger, F. N., & Pedhazur, E. J. (1973). *Multiple regression in behavioral research.* New York: Holt, Rinehart, & Winston.

Kidwell, J. S. (1981). Number of siblings, sibling spacing, sex, and birth order: Their effects on perceived parent-adolescent relationships. *Journal of Marriage and the Family, 43*(2), 315–332.

Kleck, R. E., Richardson, S. A., & Ronald L. (1974). Physical appearance cues and interpersonal attraction in children. *Child Development, 45,* 305–310.

Kogan, L., Smith, J., & Jenkins, S. (1977). Ecological validity of indicator data as predictors of survey findings. *Journal of Social Service Research, 1,* 117–132.

Koslin, S. C., Amarel, M., & Ames, N. (1970). The effect of race on peer evaluation and preference in primary grade children: An exploratory study. *Journal of Negro Education, 39*(4), 346–350.

Lago, D. J., Baskey, P., Green, C., & Hand, R. (1981). *Do pet companions help when you live alone: Content analysis of a newsletter survey.* Unpublished manuscript, Pennsylvania State University, Companion Animal Project, College of Human Development.

Lago, D., Knight, B., & Connell, C. (1982, April). *Placing companion animals in community settings: Organizational structure and operating policies in promoting health and well-being among elderly people.* Paper presented at the Third Symposium of Pets in Society, Toronto.

Lamb, M. (1978). *Social and personality development.* New York: Holt, Rinehart, & Winston.

Landy, D. (1959). *Tropical childhood.* Chapel Hill: University of North Carolina Press.

Langer, J. (1969). *Theories of development.* New York: Holt, Rinehart, & Winston.

Levinson, B. M. (1978). Pets and personality development. *Psychological Reports,* **42,** 1031–1038.

Lewin, K. (1936). *Principles of topological psychology.* New York: McGraw.

Lewin, K. (1951). *Field theory in social science: Selected theoretical papers.* New York: Harper.

Lewis, M., & Weinraub, M. (1976). The father's role in the infant's social network. In M. E. Lamb (Ed.), *The role of the father in child development.* New York: Wiley.

Liebert, R. M., Neale, J. M., & Davidson, F. S. (1973). *The early window: Effects of television on children and youth.* New York: Pergamon.

Lomnitz, L. A. (1977). *Networks and marginality: Life in a Mexican Shantytown.* New York: Academic Press.

Maccoby, E. (1961). The taking of adult roles in middle childhood. *Journal of Abnormal and Social Psychology,* **63**(3), 493–503.

MacDonald, A. J. (1979). Review: Children and companion pets. *Child: Care, Health, and Development,* **5,** 347–358.

Marcus, C. (1974). Children's play behavior in a low-rise, inner-city housing development. In D. H. Carson (Ed.), *Man-environment interactions: Evaluations and applications* (Pt. 3, pp. 197–211). New York: Wiley.

Martin, W. (1972). *Parental and interpersonal determinants of trust.* Unpublished doctoral dissertation, Emory University.

Maurer, R., & Baxter, J. C. (1972). Images of the neighborhood and city among black-, Anglo-, and Mexican-American children. *Environment and Behavior,* **4**(4), 351–388.

McCall, R. B. (1977). Challenges to a science of developmental psychology. *Child Development,* **48,** 333–344.

Mead, M. (1928). *Coming of age in Samoa.* New York: Morrow.

Medrich, E. A., Roizen, J., Rubin, U., & Buckley, S. (1982). *The serious business of growing up: A study of children's lives outside school.* Berkeley: University of California Press.

Minuchin, S. (1974). *Families and family therapy.* Cambridge, MA: Harvard University Press.

Moore, R., & Young, D. (1978). Childhood outdoors: Toward a social ecology of the landscape. In I. Altman & J. F. Wohlwill (Eds.), *Children and the environment* (pp. 83–130). New York: Plenum.

Murphy, L. B. (1962). *The widening world of childhood: Paths toward mastery.* New York: Basic.

Murphy, L. B. (1974). Coping, vulnerability, and resilience in childhood. In G. V. Coelho, D. A. Hamburg, & J. E. Adams (Eds.), *Coping and adaptation* (pp. 69–100). New York: Basic.

Murphy, L. B., & Moriarty, A. E. (1976). *Vulnerability, coping and growth: From infancy to adolescence.* New Haven, CT: Yale University Press.

Novak, D. W. (1974). Children's reactions to emotional disturbance in imaginary peers. *Journal of Consulting and Clinical Psychology,* **42**(3), 462.

Nowicki, S. (1971). *Achievement and popularity as related to locus of control across different age groups.* Unpublished manuscript, Emory University.

Nowicki, S., & Barnes, J. (1973). Effects of a structured camp experience on locus of control orientation. *Journal of Genetic Psychology,* **122,** 247–252.

Nowicki, S., & Duke, M. (1974). A preschool and primary internal-external control scale. *Developmental Psychology,* **10**(16), 874–880.

Nowicki, S., & Strickland, B. R. (1973). A locus of control scale for children. *Journal of Consulting and Clinical Psychology,* **40,** 148–154.

Piaget, J. (1932). *The moral judgment of the child.* London: Kegan Paul.

Polansky, N. A., Chalmers, M. A., Buttenwieser, E. W., & Williams, D. P. (1981). *Damaged parents: An anatomy of child neglect.* Chicago: University of Chicago Press.

Powell, E. R., & White, F. (1969). Peer-concept ratings in rural children. *Psychological Reports,* **24,** 461–462.

Proshansky, H. M., Ittelson, W. H., & Rivlin, L. G. (1972). Freedom of choice and behavior in a physical setting. In J. F. Wohlwill & D. H. Carson (Eds.), *Environment and the social sciences: Perspectives and applications*. Washington, DC: American Psychological Association.

Rapoport, L. (1962). The state of crisis: Some theoretical considerations. *Social Service Review, 36*, 22–31.

Roff, M., Sell, S. B., & Golden, M. M. (1972). *Social adjustment and personality development in children*. Minneapolis: University of Minnesota Press.

Rothenberg, B. (1970). Children's social sensitivity and the relationship to interpersonal competence, intrapersonal comfort and intellectual level. *Developmental Psychology, 2*(3), 335–350.

Rubin, Z. (1980). *Children's friendships*. Cambridge, MA: Harvard University Press.

Scarr, S. (Ed.). (1979). Psychology and children: Current research and practice [Special issue]. *American Psychologist, 34*(10).

Schwartz, B. (1968). The social psychology of privacy. *American Journal of Sociology, 73*, 741–752.

Seeman, M. (1946). A situational approach to intra-group Negro attitudes. *Sociometry, 9*, 199–206.

Smock, C. D. (1957). The relationship between "intolerance of ambiguity," generalization and speed of perceptual closure. *Child Development, 28*, 27–36.

Smock, C. D. (1958). Perceptual rigidity and closure phenomenon as a function of manifest anxiety in children. *Child Development, 29*, 237–247.

Spencer, J. (1964). *Stress and release in an urban estate*. London: Tavistock.

Stack, C. B. (1974). *All of our kin: Strategy for survival in a black community*. New York: Harper & Row.

Sullivan, H. S. (1953). *The interpersonal theory of psychiatry*. New York: Norton.

Vaillancourt, P. M. (1973). Stability of children's survey responses. *Public Opinion Quarterly, 37*(3), 373–387.

van Vliet, W. C. (1981). The environmental context of children's friendships: An empirical and conceptual examination of the role of child density. In A. E. Osterberg, C. P. Tiernan, & R. A. Findlay (Eds.), *Proceedings from the 12th annual conference of the Environmental Design Research Association* (pp. 216–224).

Viney, L. L. (1976). The concept of crisis: A tool for clinical psychologists. *Bulletin of the British Psychological Society, 29*, 387–395.

Waldrop, M. F., & Halverson, C. F. (1975). Intensive and extensive peer behavior: Longitudinal and cross-sectional analyses. *Child Development, 46*, 19–26.

Walker, K. N., MacBride, A., & Vachon, M. L. (1977). Social support networks and the crisis of bereavement. *Social Science and Medicine, 11*, 35–41.

Werner, E. E. (1979). *Cross-cultural child development: A view from the planet earth*. Monterey, CA: Brooks/Cole.

Werner, E. E., & Smith, R. S. (1977). *Kauai's children come of age*. Honolulu: University Press of Hawaii.

Werner, E. E., & Smith, R. S. (1982). *Vulnerable, but invincible: A longitudinal study of resilient children and youth*. New York: McGraw-Hill.

Werner, H. (1948). *Comparative psychology of mental development*. New York: International Universities Press.

Westin, A. F. (1967). *Privacy and freedom*. New York: Atheneum.

White, R. (1976). *The enterprise of living* (2d ed.). New York: Holt, Rinehart, & Winston.

Wolfe, M. (1978). Childhood and privacy. In I. Altman & J. F. Wohlwill (Eds.), *Children and the environment*. New York: Plenum.

Wolock, I., & Horowitz, B. (1979). Child maltreatment and material deprivation among AFDC-recipient families. *Social Service Review, 53,* 175–194.

Wright, B. A. (1960). *Physical disability: A psychological approach.* New York: Harper & Row.

Yamamoto, J., Acosta, F., & Evans, L. A. (1982). The poor and working-class patient. In F. Acosta, J. Yamamoto, & L. A. Evans (Eds.), *Effective psychotherapy for low-income and minority patients* (pp. 31–50). New York: Plenum.

Young, L. (1964). *Wednesday's children: A study of child neglect and abuse.* New York: McGraw-Hill.

Zelkowitz, P. (1978). *Children's support networks: An exploratory analysis.* Special qualifying paper, Harvard Graduate School of Education.

Zill, N. (1977). *National survey of children: Summary of preliminary results.* Unpublished manuscript, Foundation for Child Development, New York.

Zill, N. (in press). *Learning to listen to children.* New York: Cambridge University Press.

Zingale, H. Edwards, D. W., & Yarvis, R. (1978, April). *Outcome of outpatient child psychotherapy from three different perspectives: Children, parents, and therapists.* Paper presented at the annual meeting of the Western Psychological Association, San Francisco.

ACKNOWLEDGMENTS

I extend my personal thanks and appreciation to Orville Brim, president, Jane Dustan, vice-president, and the Board of Directors of the Foundation for Child Development in New York for their financial support in this project and faith in the value of listening to children. This financial support supplemented the financial support provided by the Agriculture Experiment Station, University of California, Davis. This investigation grew out of the Western Regional Project (W-144) entitled "The Development of Social Competencies in Children" and became the foundation for an ongoing Experiment Station research project entitled "Developmental Perspective of Sources of Support and Psychological Well-Being." Uri Bronfenbrenner's provocative stimulation to a naive undergraduate in a time long past as well as his more recent positive evaluation of an early proposal describing the Neighborhood Walk method is thankfully acknowledged. The feedback and encouragement generously offered to me by Lois Murphy is warmly acknowledged as well. In addition, I am also especially grateful to Nicholas Zill for his personal encouragement of my work and his generosity in sharing his own research experiences with me. Careful data collection efforts were born by Jan Hall, Halley Grain, Edna Scott, JoAnne Savage, and Jeff Parker. The enormous job of careful data coding was undertaken by Susan Burger, Doretta Garcia, Edna Scott, Diane Veevaert, Teresa Gambrell, and Liz Weber. Their ability to work together efficiently and cooperatively is a credit to their professional skills. Sherrie Graves provided data on the effects of Proposition 13. I also thank Susan Burger, Leanne Friedman, Jeff Parker, and Pat Worley for the enormous effort they gave to the challenges of data analysis. I owe a special debt to Pat Worley, Jeff Parker, and Susan Burger for their ever-present patience and goodwill as well as their ability to learn new technical skills. My gratitude is also extended to Curt Acredolo, whose statistical knowledge has enormously enhanced the quality of this report. I sincerely thank Emmy Werner, Larry Harper, Mary Jo Good, and Richard Weinberg, who provided constructive feedback and who continually expressed enthusiasm for my efforts on this project. Guy Whitlow and

Paula Heady typed this manuscript with speed and good humor in spite of deadline pressures. My most special thanks of all go to the children who participated in this study and gave me the opportunity to get to know them.

INSIGHTS FROM LISTENING TO CHILDREN

COMMENTARY BY ROSS D. PARKE

Many of the most interesting discoveries are often made at interdisciplinary boundaries. This *Monograph*, which draws on anthropology, environmental psychology, sociology, and child development, is a fine demonstration of this maxim and a fitting contribution to the *Monograph* series of an interdisciplinary society. This work deserves a broad readership. As diverse a group as epidemiologists, urban planners, sociologists, clinical and community psychologists, and students of social and emotional development will all find conceptual and empirical value in it.

Our understanding of the ecology of childhood is changing. In place of a highly limited and limiting view of children's social environment as restricted largely to parents, especially mothers, interacting with their children in the home, a new and expanded view of children's world has emerged. Not only are fathers and siblings viewed as important socialization agents, but also relationships with individuals outside the home and family are increasingly recognized as playing an important role in children's socioemotional development. This *Monograph* is both a reflection of and a contribution to our emerging reformulation of children's environments.

Let me first highlight some of the major contributions of this work. First, Bryant has forcefully shown that the concept of social network, which has been of increasing importance in studies of adult social adaptation and adjustment, is of considerable value for understanding children's development as well. Moreover, this work moves beyond earlier conceptual analyses (e.g., Cochran & Brassard, 1979) by showing the value of direct examination of children's social networks as opposed to the more usual focus on the impact of adult social networks on children (see Ladd, 1983; Zelkowitz, 1984). This work serves as a corrective to our common assumption that often limited our exploration of children's social networks themselves, namely, that children's access to extrafamilial agents or agencies is mediated by family members. As this *Monograph* suggests, access is often direct, without the mediation of adults. In part, this view grew out of the fact that the bulk of the research in the socioemotional domain was focused on infancy and early childhood, where access to social opportunities is often mediated by parents.

Second, this study makes a major contribution to our definition of social networks, by expanding the scope to include a broad range of individuals, including extended kin such as grandparents and a few unexpected confidants such as pets. The value of this expansion is clearly illustrated in this study by the fact that different members of the social network seem to serve different functions in terms of socioemotional functioning. Moreover, while no single agent in the network was highly predictive, nearly all the support agents were related to some facet of socioemotional adjustment. This suggests that future investigators need to include a wide range of sources of support in their research.

This *Monograph* represents a broadened view of social support that includes both relatedness to others and the opportunities to be autonomous of others. Too often prior conceptual work has focused solely on the former, to the neglect of the latter. However, as previous work has clearly shown, privacy is important from infancy on (Wachs & Gruen, 1982) and increases across age (Parke & Sawin, 1979). Conceptualization of social support in this dual component fashion is an important contribution.

Perhaps less successful is the unusual step of including children's intrapersonal resources as a source of support. In contrast to the other kinds of support that are environmental or interpersonal, intrapersonal skills can be viewed as either products of other kinds of support or producers of socioemotional development themselves. Broadening of support in this way may create conceptual confusion rather than clarity.

Third, the choice of middle childhood as the period of development is in itself noteworthy. As the shackles of infancy have been loosened, many researchers have leaped ahead to embrace adolescence as the new favorite period of development and in the process left a glaring gap in our knowledge of middle childhood (Collins, 1984).

By bringing a developmental orientation to this age period, Bryant has shown that there is considerable change in both the organization of socioemotional functioning and the scope and differentiation of social networks. While the finding that the coherence of different measures of socioemotional functioning for the 7-year-olds in the study was less than the coherence for the 10-year-olds yielded a less conceptually and analytically tidy package, these same differences underscored the richness of the developmental changes during this period. Moreover, it is important to highlight the dual nature of the developmental changes discovered by Bryant. Not only does the organization of the socioemotional indices shift across this relatively brief span of development, but the social structure of children's lives changes as well. The finding that children have more differentiated networks across age is especially noteworthy. The fact that 10-year-olds have a wider range of contacts than do 7-year-olds may reflect a greater access to a large number of individuals in their environment that 10-year-olds have. Or perhaps as children develop they value a wider variety of social contacts, which can satisfy their increasingly diverse social and emotional needs. This focus on both intraindividual and socioenvironmental aspects of developmental change represents a maturing of our developmental models.

At the same time that the study highlights some interesting theoretical issues, it is still the case that one of the central weaknesses of this *Monograph* is the lack of a better developed theory to guide the search and explain the findings of this project. While it can be argued that the kind of descriptive work provided by this investigation is a necessary step in theory building, more attention needs to be given to theory construction if substantial progress is going to be achieved in this area.

A theory in this area needs three aspects. First, we need a more coherent theory of social networks that not only articulates clear boundaries of whom to include but also articulates, in detail, the functions served by different network members. Second, we need a better theory of socioemotional development, one that provides a guide to which aspects are likely to show developmental shifts and how these different facets of the socioemotional domain interrelate at different ages. Bryant has provided a good empirical start on the latter issue, but now we need a better rationale for the different degrees of interrelatedness across age. The third theoretical need, namely, the linkage between social support and socioemotional development, is both the toughest and the most interesting aspect. There are two parts to this final theoretical issue. On the one hand, we need to know what aspects of socioemotional development are most likely to be influenced by social network factors. On the other hand, we need to specify the processes by which social networks influence different aspects of social development. This requires sensitive combining of the first two theoretical issues, namely, the need for better theories of both social networks and socioemotional development. This will allow us to make clearer predictions about which aspects of the social network are likely to contribute to which specific facets of social development. More important, this will help illuminate what characteristics of the relationships between the child and social network members account for these changes in development. Bryant's brief discussion of how grandparents may contribute to the development of empathy by their provision of a safe context "for exploring and acknowledging feelings of selves and others" is moving in this direction. Without further theoretical work to synthesize, organize, and predict, we may end up with an overwhelmingly complex array of empirical relationships in search of explanation. While simply less empiricism and more theory is not the answer, it is clear that this area would profit from more theory-guided empirical endeavors.

A new methodology has been identified as well that has promise for children of other ages and for eliciting information on other topics. As an alternative to the use of multiple informants, the Neighborhood Walk technique relies on the use of multiple questions and on the concreteness of specific situations that are highly familiar to the child to ensure reliable answers. It is unfortunate that no clear demonstration was provided of the superiority of the Neighborhood Walk over a regular interview. It is not yet evident that the physical "walk" aspect of the Neighborhood Walk is necessary.

One of the implicit assumptions of this approach is that we have given insufficient attention to children's perceptions of the importance of differing aspects of their environment in our enthusiasm to develop reliable and objective indices. This emphasis is consistent with recent studies (e.g., Wahler, 1980) that report that it is the perceived importance, value, or control rather than the amount of contact per se that is the important predictor in studies of the impact of social networks on adult behavior. However, this shift back to self-reports, in the interest of defining children's phenomenological views of their social world, should not mean an abandonment of the major advances in observational methodology that have been achieved over the last decade. While the test-retest reliabilities are reasonable, and predictive validity attests to the value of this approach, observations of children during the course of a typical day in the neighborhood would help convince skeptics that reliance on children's self-reports alone will be sufficient. At this point we do not yet know whether children's perceptions are better predictors than objective observations are. A comparative study of these two approaches with children of different ages would be worthwhile since it is clear that self-report approaches have limited utility with very young children. In the final analysis, the proof is in the predictive power of these approaches. Of course, they need be viewed not as incompatible but as complementary approaches to tapping possibly distinct facets of how children relate to their social environment.

There are some other limitations. The sample is highly restricted, and this may severely limit the generality of the results. The families were very stable in terms of both marital status and residential mobility and were nearly all white intact families who lived in relatively small, safe communities. In view of prior literature, which suggests that social network composition and functions vary across class, race, and size of community, unusual care has to be taken in generalizing from these findings (Bronfenbrenner, Moen, & Garbarino, 1984; Stack, 1974).

Perhaps more troublesome is the assumption that underlies the choice of a low-stress environment as a context for assessing the stress-support linkage. Bryant assumes that this study provides a baseline against which future studies of more severe forms of stress can be contrasted. However, it is unclear whether the stress of daily living encountered in a relatively secure and safe environment can or should be conceptualized as a qualitatively similar but quantitatively milder version of more severe types of either chronic or acute stress. The chronic stress of living in poverty in a relatively unsafe inner-city area may be a qualitatively different experience. Similarly, the impact of an acute stressor such as divorce, job loss, or the death of a parent or sibling may be very different. In turn, these more severe types of stress may yield different relationships to sources of support in the child's environment. These comments do not invalidate the pioneering work of this *Monograph;* they merely underscore the necessity of carefully examining our assumptions about the continuity of stressful experiences across the full range of environmental stressors.

Another limitation of the Neighborhood Walk technique is its failure to investigate reasons for the absence of particular kinds of support. A focus on the "here and now" probably increases reliability but at the same time points up one of the limitations of this approach. Consider the issue of grandparents. Their potential value may be underestimated by this tech-nique since the Neighborhood Walk approach assumes that only the agents and places that are physically accessible to the child are important. Particu-larly as children develop and are able more adequately to represent agents and events not immediately present, it is important to evaluate the impact of distal as well as proximal contacts. Grandparents are often accessible by phone or letter or are the objects of discussion. The relative importance of social support figures that are frequently accessible as opposed to those that are infrequently available needs to be addressed (see Tinsley & Parke, 1984).

This *Monograph* has policy implications as well. The results clearly dem-onstrate the value of organizing programs around existing informal social networks instead of through formal organizations. As this work demon-strates, important basic research and policy issues need not follow separate paths. Instead, well-executed research is the best basis for formulating sen-sible social policy. Kurt Lewin (1951) taught us that lesson many decades ago, and this work serves as a timely reminder. Lewin would be pleased!

In closing, this *Monograph* is a major contribution to our understanding of the links between children's social networks and their socioemotional development, an innovative methodological advance, and an invitation to others to tackle the difficult but fruitful task of studying children in their natural environments.

References

Bronfenbrenner, U., Moen, P., & Garbarino, J. (1984). Child, family, and community. In R. D. Parke, R. N. Emde, H. P. MacAdoo, & G. P. Sackett (Eds.), *The family* (pp. 283–328). Chicago: University of Chicago Press.

Cochran, M. M., & Brassard, J. A. (1979). Child development and personal social networks. *Child Development, 50,* 601–616.

Collins, W. A. (Ed.). (1984). *Development during middle childhood: The years six to twelve.* Washington, DC: National Academy Press.

Ladd, G. W. (1983). Social networks of popular, average and rejected children in school settings. *Merrill-Palmer Quarterly, 29,* 282–307.

Lewin, K. (1951). *Field theory in social science: Selected theoretical papers.* New York: Harper.

Parke, R. D., & Sawin, D. B. (1979). Children's privacy in the home: Developmental, ecological, and child-rearing determinants. *Environment and Behavior, 11,* 87–104.

Stack, C. (1974). *All our kin.* New York: Harper & Row.

Tinsley, B., & Parke, R. D. (1984). Grandparents as support and socialization agents. In M. Lewis (Ed.), *Beyond the dyad* (pp. 161–194). New York: Plenum.

Wachs, T. D., & Gruen, G. E. (1982). *Early experience and human development.* New York: Plenum.

Wahler, R. G. (1980). Parental insularity as a determinant of generalization success in family treatment. In S. Salzinger, J. Antrobus, & O. J. Glick (Eds.), *The ecosystem of the "sick" child* (pp. 187–200). New York: Academic Press.

Zelkowitz, P. (1984, August). *Comparing maternal and child reports of children's social networks.* Paper presented at the meeting of the American Psychological Association, Toronto.

[**Ross D. Parke** (Ph.D. 1965, University of Waterloo) is professor of psychology at the University of Illinois at Urbana-Champaign. He is the author of *Fathers* (1981); coauthor, with E. M. Hetherington, of *Child psychology: A contemporary perspective* (3d ed., in press); editor, with R. N. Emde, H. P. McAdoo, & G. P. Sackett, of *The family*, Review of Child Development Research, Vol. **7** (1984); and editor-elect of *Developmental Psychology.* His research interests are focused on families, especially on the role of the father in social development.]